Dedicated

To the ones who remember

even when the world forgets.

To the hearts that still ache without knowing why

and to the souls that still dream across lifetimes.

To the breath that never abandoned you.

To the light that was never outside you.

To the silent language between all beings, speaking in every sunrise and every tear.

And above all

to Life itself,

in its raw, unfinished, burning perfection.

May you find your way home through these pages.

Table of Contents:

Chapter 1:

The First Crack in Reality The Illusion of Experience and the Awakening of Perception

There is a moment—often missed, almost always misunderstood—when reality is not something happening outside, but something being constructed within.

This moment doesn't announce itself.

It slides beneath your awareness.

And yet it is the true beginning of your life. Not the life you were told to live—but the one that sees itself.

When you were born, the world did not imprint itself upon you like a stamp on wax.

You absorbed it through sensation—yes.

But sensation, without awareness, is just chaos.

So your mind began to organize.

It wrapped light into meaning.

It called pain "bad" and warmth "mother."

And in doing so, it laid the first brick in a house you would one day mistake for the universe.

The Sensory Illusion

What if I told you your senses are not trustworthy? Not because they're faulty—but because they are ***loyal*** to your survival, not to your truth.

Your ears hear what they are trained to hear.

Your eyes scan not for what is, but for what matters to your story.

Touch, taste, smell—they all report to a nervous system that is more invested in ***confirmation*** than ***contemplation***.

This means what you call "reality" is not real. It is a rendering.

A filtered echo of a deeper, chaotic presence—shaped, softened, and sharpened into something tolerable.

This is not deception.

It is design.

But the danger comes when you forget the difference.

Meaning Is Memory

By the time you were three years old, you had already built a version of the world that you would spend decades reinforcing.

And like a loyal servant, your brain complied.

It painted everything new with the brush of the familiar.

Even love. Even failure. Even God.

The smell of a room. The tone of a voice.

Everything began to form feedback loops—

and you started living not through presence, but through ***pattern recognition***.

You stopped seeing.

You started recalling.

And this is the first crack in reality.

Not when the illusion appears—

But when you mistake it for what is.

The Mind As Projector

You were taught your mind is a mirror.

But this is false. It is a **projector**.

It casts outward the shapes and shadows you fear the most, then invites you to call them "reality."

Have you ever felt rejected before anyone said a word?

Have you ever felt danger in a room that was perfectly quiet?

That's not intuition. That's conditioning.

The wound remembers.

The nervous system replicates.

And reality becomes autobiographical.

You are not perceiving truth.

You are perceiving your version of it.

And unless that version is questioned, you are not free.

Awakening Begins in Doubt

The first spiritual moment is not bliss.

It is **doubt**.

Not the doubt of depression. The doubt of unlearning.

When you begin to ask:

What if this thing I've been calling "me" is not the center of the world?

What if my suffering is not a punishment—but a signal that my perception is rigged?

This doubt shakes you.

Because it threatens the foundation of your story.

But this is the doorway.

You begin to step out of the cage—and realize you built the cage.

You named it.

You colored it.

You fortified it with memory and called it logic.

But now, it starts to crack.

And you feel something rise—something terrifying and beautiful:

space.

Between Thought and Experience

There is a moment, just before a thought forms, where awareness is pure.

Not silent. Not empty. Just **clear**.

In that moment, there is no story.

No name.

No goal.

Just the living presence of now.

This moment cannot be held.

It can only be noticed.

And the more you notice it, the more it expands.

You begin to realize:

You are not your thoughts.

You are the space in which thoughts occur.

And in that realization, a fracture appears in the illusion.

The crack grows.

The Collapse of the Identity Loop

Most people don’t fear death.

They fear losing their identity.

But identity is not stable. It is a loop of feedback.

Others treat you as "you," so you respond as "you."

You succeed, so you become "the successful one."

You fail, so you carry shame.

And every time you perform your role, the loop strengthens.

But here's the truth:

You are not a loop.

You are the field beneath it.

The field that allows the loop to exist, but does not collapse into it.

When this realization hits, there is grief.

But also liberation.

Because now—finally—you can stop performing.

And start **witnessing**.

Reality After the Crack

What happens after the crack forms?

First: confusion.

Then: stillness.

Then: clarity that doesn't speak in language.

You start to see the Ramayana not as a story, but as a *map of consciousness*.

Rama is not a man. He is your inner order.

Sita is not a woman. She is the *pure awareness* abducted by ego.

Ravana is the mind that split into ten heads—all claiming to be the master.

Mahabharata becomes your karmic loop.

Every character is you—at war with yourself.

And Krishna is the inner witness, waiting patiently for you to stop collapsing into roles.

You start to see the world not as fixed—but as **fractal**.

Not as cruel—but as echoing your own frequency.

And that is when the crack turns into an opening.

Why This Crack Matters

Without this crack, there is no awakening.

Without awakening, perception remains poisoned.

And poisoned perception creates a poisoned world.

Mental health pandemics.

Disconnection.

Addiction to identity.

Technology used as escape, not expansion.

The planet isn't dying because of carbon.

It's dying because of *confused consciousness.*

This crack—this philosophical break—is not optional.

It is the only way back.

You Are Not the Wall. You Are the Window.

When you realize this, something releases inside you.

You no longer grip your story with fear.

You become curious.

You become soft.

You become available to something higher than logic—

but deeper than emotion.

You become **presence**.

And presence **melts the loop**.

This is the first crack in reality.

It's not an end.

It is your first true beginning.

Welcome.

You are now awake.

Chapter 2 :

Perception Is Not Proof The Mirror That Lies

If your eyes could speak honestly, they would say:

"I am not showing you truth—I am showing you habit."

This chapter is not about sight. It is about the ***filter that calls itself vision***.

And how your mind makes meaning faster than your awareness can catch it.

Seeing Without Understanding

Perception is not the act of seeing what is.

It is the reaction to what has already been named.

Before light enters your eyes, your brain is already guessing what it wants to see.

Before a sound reaches your ears, your nervous system has already labeled it as threat, love, or irrelevance.

What you call the "present moment" is often just the ***confirmation of your past assumptions***.

You don’t experience reality.

You experience ***what you believe reality should be***.

This is not insight.

It is a spiritual emergency.

Why Your Brain Favors Familiarity

The human brain is not built to tell the truth.

It is built to **predict**.

If something looks, sounds, or feels like something you’ve encountered before, your nervous system responds as if it is the same thing.

Why?

Because prediction is faster than presence.

It keeps you alive—but it also ***keeps you blind***.

This is how trauma loops are born.

Not just from pain—but from **recognition**.

Recognition says, "I've seen this before. React now."

But reality whispers, "This is not what you think."

And in that mismatch, suffering begins.

The Prison of Pattern

Have you ever walked into a room and felt rejected—before anyone said a word?

That is perception, not proof.

You weren't reading truth. You were ***reading memory***.

A tone of voice that sounded like an old argument.

A look that echoed a past betrayal.

A silence that reminded your nervous system of being unwanted.

These aren't facts.

These are refractions.

You are not perceiving the moment.

You are reliving it through **emotional déjà vu**.

This is the prison of perception:

You believe you are present,

but you are standing inside a ***hall of mirrors***, mistaking your reflection for reality.

The Loop Reinforces Itself

What happens when you keep trusting these illusions?

You reinforce the world as you already believe it to be.

You start choosing people who match your patterns.

You find roles that confirm your story.

You interpret kindness as manipulation, truth as threat, freedom as danger.

And then, ironically, you say:

"See? I knew it would turn out this way."

But that wasn't fate.

That was **feedback**.

Life reflects your lens.

You are not reacting to life.

You are reacting to your **version** of it.

Discomfort Is Not Always Danger

One of the greatest awakenings is this:

Discomfort does not mean danger.

Sometimes, discomfort means **truth is stretching your frame**.

Sometimes, what feels like rejection is just unfamiliar safety.

Sometimes, what feels like chaos is just **clarity dismantling your false order**.

But if your lens is cracked by fear,

you will never allow newness to enter.

You will sabotage peace because it doesn't feel "right"—

not realizing "right" is just what you're used to.

This is why perception cannot be trusted as proof.

Because it is often the echo of a wound, not the arrival of wisdom.

Cleaning the Lens

So how do you begin to see clearly?

Not by trusting the eyes.

Not by analyzing every thought.

But by watching—**without attaching**.

The goal is not to eliminate perception.

It is to become aware of the projector.

Imagine stepping outside your mind's loop for just one second—

and noticing the gap between the stimulus and your reaction.

In that space, you gain power.

You see the filter forming.

You can say: "This reaction is not me. It is my pattern."

And when you name the pattern,

you break its spell.

Presence Beyond Perception

There is a way of being that does not depend on confirmation.

It's not blind trust.

It's **presence without proof**.

It means letting someone love you, even when your old self says,

"Love is manipulation."

It means sitting in silence without calling it loneliness.

It means not assuming the worst, even if the worst has happened before.

This isn't naivety.

It is **radical clarity**.

You stop believing every thought.

You stop defending every fear.

You stop needing proof for every step.

And you realize:

Perception is a tool—not a truth.

The Wisdom of Doubt

Here's the paradox:

To see clearly, you must first **doubt what you see**.

You must doubt the emotional reflex.

Doubt the conditioned reaction.

Doubt the story that screams in your head before the moment even unfolds.

This doubt is not despair.

It is **awakening**.

Because once you know your mind is sculpting your world,

you become an artist instead of a victim.

You start painting with awareness instead of trauma.

And the world begins to respond to your clarity.

When You See Without Needing To Be Right

Most people do not want truth.

They want to be right.

Even if that "rightness" means more suffering.

They would rather feel familiar than feel free.

But when perception is no longer your proof,
you stop needing to win.
You stop needing to defend your reality.

You become humble.
Curious.
Available.

And in that softness, **clarity floods in**.

This clarity cannot be argued with.
Because it is not a thought.
It is a state of being.

So let this land:

What you perceive is not what is.

It is what your system is trained to notice.

You don't need to fight your mind.

You just need to witness it—and not obey.

Then, reality begins to show itself.

Not through fear.

Not through story.

But through ***presence***.

Through ***resonance***.

Through the quiet knowing beneath all reactions.

That knowing has no need for proof.

Because it is already home.

Chapter 3:

Memory as the Architect of the Present The Unseen Sculptor of Reality

The present moment is rarely present.

We speak of "now" as if we're living in it, breathing in it, grounded in its clarity.

But beneath every action, reaction, emotion, or belief, there is a ghost.

That ghost has a name: ***memory***.

Memory is not a passive archive.

It is an architect—designing your thoughts, your reactions, your identity, and your experience.

It does not live in the past.

It is **invisibly shaping your present**.

The Past Is Not Behind You

The greatest illusion humans hold is that the past is behind them.

It is not.

It is **inside you**.

Every choice you make, every person you trust or avoid, every emotion you feel in response to silence or chaos—it is all filtered through **accumulated memory**.

When someone says something that hurts,

is it their voice that wounds you,

or the echo of a parent who said the same thing 20 years ago?

When a moment feels unsafe,

is it because danger is present,

or because your nervous system learned to expect danger when things go quiet?

This is how memory becomes ***architecture***.

It builds your reality before you even open your eyes.

You Don't Respond to What Is—You Respond to What Was

When someone looks at you with a certain expression,

your reaction isn't to that expression—

it's to ***everything your system has associated with that look***.

Raised eyebrows?

Maybe in your memory, that meant judgment.

Slight irritation?

Maybe that used to precede abandonment.

So now, in the present moment, your body prepares for rejection, not because rejection is happening—

but because ***your memory said it might***.

The body becomes the memory's loyal servant.

And your reality becomes a shadow play of your past.

Memory Isn't Recollection—It's Repetition

You think of memory as stored moments.

But more often, memory is a **set of automated responses**.

It is a code, silently running in your background.

It predicts. It protects. It possesses.

Your sense of identity? Memory.

Your sense of worth? Memory.

Your fears, desires, and even your idea of God?

All shaped by emotional memories—some conscious, most not.

This is why the present is so rare.

Because most of us aren't living—we're ***looping***.

You Were Not Born With a Name

Before memory taught you who you were, you were something else.

You were not your name.

Not your gender.

Not your culture, your trauma, or your talents.

You were presence.

You were witness.

You were vibration.

But memory wrapped itself around you like skin.

It told you what to expect, how to act, what to defend.

And now, most of what you call "you" is simply a long-running file of remembered scripts.

You are not broken.

You are just repeating too much.

The Emotional Reflex Is Not Truth

One of the clearest signs that memory is running your present is the **emotional reflex**.

Someone says something—and your heart rate jumps.

You feel unexplainable dread before a conversation.

You react with anger before understanding the moment.

This is not sensitivity.

It is **conditioned memory**.

You are not choosing your reaction.

You are reliving one.

And unless you bring this into awareness,

you will mistake your nervous system for your intuition.

Integration, Not Erasure

Spiritual traditions often speak of dissolving the past.

But let's be clear—you cannot delete memory.

What you can do is update its influence.

You don't need to forget.

You need to disobey.

When the old fear rises,

you don't run—you breathe.

When the shame echoes,

you don't collapse—you observe.

When the identity begins to perform,

you don't fight it—you smile and step aside.

This is not denial.

It is integration.

Memory loses its grip the moment you stop believing it is you.

Memory and the Identity Loop

The identity you protect is memory's child.

Who are you if not "the achiever"?

Who are you if not "the unloved one"?

Who are you if not "the strong one" who hides their feelings?

These aren't truths.

They are **roles** memory cast you in.

And the moment you stop playing the part,

memory panics.

It says, "Wait, if you're not this, then who are you?"

And that fear—the fear of the unknown self—is what keeps people stuck.

But the truth is this:

You were never the part.

You were the ***stage***.

You were the space on which the memory performed.

You were always free.

Breaking the Predictive Cycle

If you want to reclaim your present moment,

you must challenge the **predictive cycle**.

The mind says,

"I know how this will go."

But awareness says,

"Let's find out."

This shift—from prediction to presence—breaks the architecture.

It takes courage.

Because it feels like death.

The death of what you thought you knew.

The death of who you thought you were.

But what remains is real.

Untouched. Untrained. Alive.

You.

Memory as Teacher, Not Tyrant

When memory is no longer the architect,

it becomes the **oracle**.

You see the patterns—not as prisons,

but as **clues** to your own becoming.

The childhood wound no longer defines you.

It informs your empathy.

The old failure no longer haunts you.

It teaches precision.

The heartbreak no longer closes you.

It shapes your depth.

This is how memory evolves:

from tyrant to **teacher**.

Reclaiming the Present

So pause.

Right now, feel this moment without naming it.

Not through your past.

Not through your habits.

Just... here.

No role.

No history.

No defense.

This space—this unfiltered presence—

is what your memory has tried to protect you from.

Because it is vast.

It is unknown.

It is **freedom**.

You were never meant to live in memory.

You were meant to live in rhythm with life itself.

And life only happens now.

Chapter 4:

The Myth of Control and the Fractal of Chaos Where the Mind Breaks, and the Cosmos Breathes

You are not in control.

And you never were.

You were taught that control is power. That effort leads to reward. That planning equals protection.

But this chapter is not about managing life.

This chapter is about remembering that the controller is a memory, a reaction, a frightened mind pretending to be the divine.

Control is not strength.

It is the last gasp of identity before it dissolves into cosmic rhythm.

The Beginning of the Myth

The first lie you were told was that you are separate.

The second was that, because you are separate, you must control what is outside you to survive.

This lie becomes the architecture of your reality.

Your body tenses. Your thoughts tighten. You mistake planning for presence.

You build goals, schedules, expectations, and habits—

Not because they are inherently wrong,

but because they are attempts to escape uncertainty.

But life was never uncertain.

Only your ego is.

Life is pure rhythm. Chaos is not disorder. It is order the ego cannot predict.

Control Is Not Consciousness

You believe you're controlling your life.

But what if the you doing the controlling is a program of memory, fear, and inherited patterns?

Control is the software of the frightened identity.

And so, every time you say,

"I must make this happen,"

what you really mean is:

"I am terrified that if I surrender, I will dissolve."

And yes—you will.

Not into failure.

But into truth.

When the Controller Cracks

There will be a moment, if you are blessed, when your control collapses.

The job falls apart.

The relationship disappears.

The health slips.

The plans burn.

You scream, "Why is this happening?"

But beneath that scream is a whisper:

"This is your release."

Because what dies when control fails is your false self.

And what is born is the witness.

The Feedback Loop of False Power

The controller feeds itself.

It says, "If I predict, I am safe."

"If I manage others, I am worthy."

"If I avoid chaos, I am intelligent."

But this is a feedback loop, not freedom.

"The controller is a self-reinforcing function of fear disguised as responsibility."

It doesn't seek truth. It seeks familiarity.

It doesn't serve your soul. It serves your trauma.

This loop must break.

Not because it is evil—

but because it cannot carry you into awareness.

Ramayana: The Exile of Order

In the Ramayana, Rama is order. He is dharma embodied.

But he is exiled—not by failure, but by fate.

Why?

Because even the archetype of perfection must lose control to realize divinity.

Rama doesn't resist the chaos of exile.

He walks it.

Through forests, demons, loss, and longing.

He does not command reality. He submits to its wisdom.

This is not defeat.

This is cosmic alignment.

The soul does not conquer the world.

The soul dances within it.

Mahabharata: The Fractal of Conflict

The Mahabharata is not just a war. It is a mirror of internal fragmentation.

The Pandavas are not saints.

The Kauravas are not villains.

They are loops. Echoes. Splits of consciousness playing out on a karmic chessboard.

Each generation believes they can control the outcome.

Each one fails.

Because the war is not between families—

it is between will and wisdom.

Krishna speaks to Arjuna not as a commander, but as a witness:

"You were never the doer. Drop the illusion."

This is your teaching:

Karma is a fractal.

Until you surrender, the pattern repeats.

What Chaos Really Is

Chaos is not destruction.

It is depth.

It is the layer beneath surface logic.

It is the voice of the universal pattern breaking your personal plan.

You fear it because it cannot be tamed.

But it can be heard.

Chaos is when the mind lets go, and the cosmos starts speaking.

The spiral of galaxies.

The split in your plans.

The ache that makes no sense.

All of it is language.

Not error—design.

You Are Not the Doer

"I do not exist as a commander of life. I exist as its channel."

The doer is the mask.

The channel is the self.

To walk this path is not to abandon action,

but to stop believing that action defines you.

You do not act.

You align.

The Architecture of Surrender

Real surrender is not collapse.

It is coherence.

It's when your breath syncs with timing.

Your intention loosens.

Your vision becomes listening instead of striving.

You become available instead of assertive.

You don't command the wave.

You surf it.

Surrender is not weakness.

It is participation in the larger intelligence.

The Cosmic Paradox

Here is the paradox you must embody:

You must act, yet not grasp.

You must choose, yet know the choice is unfolding.

You must walk the path, knowing the path is walking you.

This is not a contradiction.

It is the heartbeat of the universe.

And the only way to feel it

is to stop trying to control the rhythm

and become the rhythm.

What Follows the Death of Control

When you release the illusion of control:

Peace arrives—but not the kind you imagined.

Silence speaks—not with answers, but with awareness.

Life doesn't get easier.

It gets true.

And in that truth,

you are not smaller—

you are infinite.

You stop being the mind trying to master the pattern.

You become the pattern remembering itself.

Control Is the Dream. Chaos Is the Awakening.

Everything you feared losing was never yours.

The controller was dreaming.

The soul was waiting.

And now—through this crack—

you remember the truth:

You were never the storm.

You were the sky it danced in.

You were never meant to control the fractal.

You were meant to become it.

Chapter 5:

The Architecture of the False Self How Illusion Builds Identity and Identity Builds the World

The greatest trick ever performed was not by a magician—

It was by the **human mind**,

which convinced you that you exist as a separate, defined self.

You call it "**I**."

You protect it. You defend it. You grieve for it. You build monuments around it.

But this "**I**" is not the essence. It is the architecture of adaptation.

And in this chapter, we reveal the full blueprint of the false self—

Not to shame it, but to understand it, so that what is real may finally breathe.

You Were Born Without a Name

Before they gave you a name, you were not missing anything.

You were breath.

You were sensation.

You were openness.

But the moment they said, "This is you,"

a construction began.

A "self" was shaped—not from the soul outward,

but from the outside inward.

And like all architecture, it had parts:

Memory (of what was praised or punished)

Labels (of who you were allowed to be)

Beliefs (about safety, love, purpose)

Rules (for survival in the tribe)

Repetition (to anchor identity through behavior)

The result?

Not a person. **A persona**.

Not consciousness**. A configuration**.

Identity Is a Feedback Loop

You were not taught to be yourself.

You were taught to become **predictable**.

And so the identity loop begins:

You do something → the world reacts → you adjust → they accept → you repeat.

What was once spontaneous now becomes **scripted**.

And every repetition deepens the **loop**.

The "**self**" becomes a habit,

a mask of impressions continuously reinforced by society's mirror.

You are not being you.

You are being who others expect you to be.

And because the reflection is consistent,

you start to believe it's true.

But the truth?

What you call "**me**" is just a highly refined **survival mechanism**.

The Role of Emotional Architecture

Your emotions were also trained.

Not felt—trained.

If you cried and were ignored,

you learned to suppress pain.

If you laughed and were praised,

you learned to perform joy.

Each emotion became a signal—not of your truth,

but of what was acceptable to express.

This is how the emotional self is built—not as truth, but as compliance.

You learned not to feel, but to signal safety.

This performance became subconscious.

And now?

You say, "I feel sad"—but it's not sadness.

It's the permissioned version of sadness.

The false self doesn't just control behavior—

It recolors your feelings, too.

The Mind Becomes the Architect

The mind is not evil.

But it believes in architecture.

It loves boundaries. Shapes. Categories. Control.

And so it builds a castle around your identity.

Every thought becomes a brick.

Every fear becomes a wall.

Every success becomes a tower.

Every failure becomes a locked room.

Eventually, you are living inside yourself—

But not your soul.

Inside your mind's idea of who you are.

And like a king who forgets he's dreaming,

you begin to rule the world from a prison of your own design.

False Self = Fragmented Memory Loop

Let’s go deeper.

The false self is not even a singular illusion.

It is a fractured mosaic made of unresolved memory.

Each trauma split you.

Each shame disowned a part of you.

Each disappointment buried a truth.

And instead of integrating, you adapted.

Instead of healing, you compensated.

So now you live in pieces:

The achiever who hides insecurity

The caretaker who suppresses needs

The rebel who's afraid of tenderness

The wise one who never felt seen as a child

This mosaic is what the world claps for.

But it is not you.

It is your intelligence protecting you from your wounds.

The Spiritual Path Is Not Self-Improvement

Here's the trap:

You awaken to the illusion, and the false self rebrands itself as "the spiritual self."

You meditate. You read. You talk about energy.

But often, it's the same identity—now wearing light instead of shadow.

Real awakening is not adding more identity.

It is dismantling the structure, beam by beam.

This is not a project.

It is a disappearance.

A death—not of life, but of pretense.

And only then...

can something unarchitected emerge.

Who Builds the False Self?

Not just culture.

Not just parents.

Not just trauma.

It is the mind trying to be safe.

The root fear is not rejection.

The root fear is formlessness.

The ego cannot survive without identity.

So it builds. It defends. It collects. It compares.

It says: "Better the prison I know than the sky I don't."

But awareness?

Awareness was never afraid.

Awareness is not a structure.

It is the field before the structure.

You were never the house.

You are the space it was built inside.

You Don't Destroy the False Self. You See Through It.

Many believe they must "**break the ego**."

But that is ego again—**trying to conquer itself**.

Truth requires no war.

When you shine light on a shadow,

you don't fight it.

You just see it.

Same with the false self.

You don't demolish.

You disidentify.

You say:

"That voice in my head is not me."

"That fear of not being enough is a script, not a soul."

"That role I've played—I can step out now."

And with that seeing,

the castle of illusion begins to fade into transparency.

The Real Self Is Not Another Identity

The real you cannot be described.

It can only be felt.

It is not a role.

Not a title.

Not a personality type.

Not even your thoughts or feelings.

It is presence before all of that.

Stillness beneath all motion.

Witness behind the actor.

You don't become it.

You remember it.

And in remembering,

you stop confusing mirrors for meaning.

Living Without the Architecture

When the false self fades, you may feel naked.

Lost. Empty.

Good.

That emptiness is not absence.

It is availability.

For the first time, you can meet the moment without performing.

You can love without role.

Speak without agenda.

Act without defending a mask.

You stop asking, "**Who am I**?"

And you begin living as:

I Am.

No prefix.

No architecture.

Just awareness, embodied.

And from there,

everything real begins.

Chapter 6:

The Echo Chamber of Thought

There is a strange prison, so invisible that most never realize they live inside it.

It is not made of walls.

It is not made of iron.

It is made of echoes —

the mind talking to itself, believing it has heard the truth.

Thought arises.

Then thought reflects upon itself.

And then thought answers its own reflection.

A loop is born.

A loop so seamless that it feels like reality.

But it is not reality.

It is a self-echoing chamber,

where your own ideas bounce back at you

wearing different masks —

disguised as facts, disguised as instincts, disguised as certainty.

The mind does not like emptiness.

So it fills the silence with commentary.

It cannot sit in the rawness of a moment.

It must name it.

Judge it.

Explain it.

Frame it inside familiar walls.

In doing so, it kills the very life of the moment.

You don't see the flower.

You see the word "flower."

You don't feel the breath.

You analyze breathing.

You don't live the mystery.

You narrate it to yourself, faster than you can experience it.

And in that narration, you move further away from life.

The echo chamber is comforting.

It gives the illusion of control.

It tells you:

"I understand.

I know who I am.

I know what the world is."

But it is a brittle knowing.

It is a glass palace that cracks the moment true mystery presses against it.

Real life — unfiltered life — is too wild, too vast, too unmanageable for the thinking mind.

And so the mind does what it must:

It loops inside its own reflections to feel safe.

Most people live their whole lives inside this echo.

They argue.

They dream.

They love.

They despair —

all within the same closed chamber of assumptions built long ago.

Rarely do they question:

"Whose voice is this in my head?

Where did these ideas come from?

Am I thinking — or am I only echoing?"

They do not ask — because asking would shatter the walls.

And for most, security feels more urgent than freedom.

But for some —the crack begins.

You start noticing the repetition.

The familiarity of your own reactions.

The smallness of your conclusions.

You start seeing that what you call "my beliefs" were planted long before you could choose them.

You start hearing the hollow ring of the echo.

And you realize:

You are not your thoughts.

You are the space in which they arise.

To break the echo chamber, you do not need better thoughts.

You need less noise.

You need to allow spaces between the thoughts to grow larger, wider and freer.

You need to stand still inside yourself —

even when the mind shouts and thrashes —

and listen not to the words,

but to the silence beneath them.

Truth does not echo.

It does not repeat slogans.

It arrives quietly — once the shouting fades.

Truth does not argue.

It does not need to convince.

It is simply seen when the mirrors stop reflecting back your own noise.

Step beyond the chamber.

Let thought arise — but do not build a home inside it.

Let ideas pass — but do not chain yourself to them.

You are not here to live inside commentary.

You are here to touch the raw, burning, wordless aliveness of being.

You are not the echo.

You are the vastness that was never touched by sound.

And in that vastness,

you remember:

you were never trapped.

Only dreaming.

Chapter 7:

Truth Is Not an Opinion

The moment you make truth an opinion, it fractures.

Not because truth is fragile,

but because the lens through which it is seen has already chosen distortion.

Opinion is not perception.

It is interpretation pretending to be perception.

And interpretation always carries the burden of the interpreter—

not the light, but the fog.

Truth does not need defense.

It does not require consensus.

It does not ask for agreement.

It exists in the absence of all projection.

It is not born through thought.

It is revealed through the silence between thoughts.

Truth is not owned.

It is witnessed.

And the one who tries to own it becomes the furthest from it.

To say "*this is my truth*" is a misstep.

There is no such thing.

There is only your experience.

And your experience may carry reflections of truth,

shadows of truth,

metaphors of truth—

but not truth itself.

Truth is not plural.
It is not personal.
It is not emotional.

It does not shift with mood,
or mutate with culture,
or bend to preference.

It is what remains when all preference dissolves.

The ego claims truth to stabilize identity.
It holds a position,
not because it knows,
but because not knowing threatens its form.

And so opinion is born—
not from clarity,
but from **insecurity** wearing **certainty's** mask.

What begins as exploration becomes fixation.

What begins as curiosity becomes ideology.

And ideology, no matter how noble,

is the crystallization of thought around a **fear of dissolution**.

Truth does not fear dissolution.

It is dissolution.

It is what exists beyond the identity that needs to be right.

It does not seek to validate the thinker.

It annihilates the thinker's need to validate.

In the presence of truth, there is no one left to defend it.

There is only awareness—

still, whole, wordless.

When two people argue about truth,

neither is standing in it.

Truth has no opposite.

It is not part of a polarity.

It is the field in which polarity arises and collapses.

It cannot be won.

It cannot be voted on.

It cannot be improved.

It can only be seen—

or missed.

And it is often missed because it arrives as quiet,

as simplicity,

as what does not serve the narrative of self.

Science seeks repeatability.

Philosophy seeks coherence.

Politics seeks power.

***Culture seeks cohesion*.**

But truth seeks nothing.

And so it is **overlooked** by all the seekers.

The scientist who needs results to match funding,

the philosopher who needs logic to win arguments,

the activist who needs ideology to form identity—

all of them may glimpse truth,

but few remain naked in its light.

Because to remain,

one must shed position.

One must unname what is seen.

One must sit in the burning clarity of "I do not know,"

long enough for knowing to dawn unannounced.

Truth is not a concept.

It is an event.

Not an event in time,

but in presence.

It does not unfold across hours.

It reveals itself in an instant—

when time collapses,

when separation dissolves,

when attention becomes still.

You do not reach truth through steps.

You fall into it through surrender.

What prevents this fall is not ignorance.

It is identification with what one believes they know.

Knowledge becomes a wall against truth when it is clung to.

The more you know, the harder it is to hear.

Because truth is not the accumulation of information.

It is the erasure of noise.

It is the simplicity left when belief and disbelief both vanish.

You will not find truth in a debate.

You will not find it in the agreement of the crowd.

You will not find it in the echo of your preference.

You will find it in the moment the self has no commentary left.

In that moment, clarity dawns.

Not as a thought,

but as seeing.

Not as possession,

but as revelation.

This is why truth cannot be taught.

It can only be pointed to.

And the finger that points must disappear.

The teacher who says "I have it" is already in error.

The sage is not one who speaks the truth,

but one whose presence no longer interferes with it.

The mouth may open,

but it speaks from emptiness.

Not from position.

Not from agenda.

Just from what-is.

And what-is is always simple.

But never small.

The mind calls truth subtle because it is not dramatic.

The heart calls truth heavy because it dismantles comfort.

The body calls truth silence because it calms all inner war.

And the soul calls truth home—

because it is what was never apart to begin with.

In a world addicted to preference,

truth sounds like a threat.

But in a heart ready to dissolve,

it arrives like liberation.

It is the final clarity—

the one that leaves nothing more to say.

Chapter 8:

The Theatre of Comparison

The moment comparison enters, presence exits.

Not because presence is fragile,

but because comparison creates a stage—

and presence does not perform.

Comparison turns life into theatre.

Not the theatre of beauty,

but the theatre of measurement.

The soul does not measure.

It moves.

It flows.

It burns.

But it does not compare.

Because it knows:

comparison is fiction layered on truth.

And fiction must be performed to survive.

The mind loves measurement.

It mistakes it for meaning.

But there is no truth in scale.

You are not better than the tree.

You are not ahead of the bird.

You are not behind the crowd.

You are not more awake than your neighbor.

You are simply here, until you are not.

And that is enough.

Enough to be real.

Enough to be free.

The ego hates "enough."

It needs "more."

And so it builds a world where everything must be weighed.

Intelligence, beauty, love, worth, awakening—

it turns qualities into contests.

The sacred becomes scoreboard.

The moment becomes market.

The inner becomes image.

Not what is felt, but what is seen.

Not what is lived, but what is ranked.

You are told you are behind.

Behind whom?

Behind what?

Behind a timeline built by people who do not know your rhythm,

do not know your pain,

do not know your contract with the Infinite.

And yet you carry their clock.

You wear their pace.

You chase their mile-markers.

And in that chase, you forget the path you never took.

Not because you were lost, but because you were **distracted**.

Comparison is not born from vision.

It is born from **insecurity**—

amplified by mirrors that do not reflect, only distort.

The world does not **compare** you.

Your **mind** does.

And when it does, you begin to perform.

You smile when you are empty.

You post when you are broken.

You praise others through gritted teeth.

You wear masks layered over masks.

The more you pretend, the more you feel unseen.

Because you are.

Even by yourself.

The real self is not afraid to be last.

Because it is not trying to be first.

It is not afraid to be small.

Because it has never believed in size.

It is not afraid to be missed.

Because it knows: **visibility is not validation**.

To exist is enough.

To breathe is miracle.

To be, without theatre, is revolution.

Comparison kills joy.

Not by taking joy away.

But by replacing it with **calculation**.

It **whispers**, "You are happy... but look at them."

And suddenly happiness turns to lack.

The food is not enough.

The home is not enough.

The relationship is not enough.

The self is not enough.

Not because anything changed—

but because someone else was seen.

This is the game of the echo world.

A world where you **only** know who you are by measuring who you are not.

And in that measurement, you become numb.

Because every gain breeds new fear.

Every success births a new scale.

And even when you win, you lose—

because you must now defend the win.

And peace dies under defense.

There is **no peace** in the theatre of comparison.

Only applause.

And applause fades.

So **the actor must perform again**.

Louder, brighter, faster.

Until there is no actor left.

Only performance.

Only exhaustion.

Only the hollow echo of claps that never reached the heart.

Step off the stage.

Leave the theatre.

Not in protest, but in presence.

You do not need to prove anything.

Your breath is not a ranking.

Your being is not a race.

Your worth is not measured by proximity to someone else's illusion.

Look at a tree.

It does not grow to outgrow another.

It does not reach toward light to block someone else.

It simply grows.

In its time.

In its curve.

In its silent agreement with nature.

You, too, are allowed to grow like this.

Without comparison.

Without theatre.

Without noise.

Comparison is a trick of thought.

A trick to make you forget what you are.

And what are you?

You are life.

Not more, not less.

Just this—conscious, unmeasured, whole.

The moment you stop measuring, you start seeing.

And what you see is not a ladder.

It is a field.

Infinite.

Without center.

Without edges.

Without rank.

Just being, meeting being.

This is freedom.

Not from others—

but from the voice that told you others were ever a threat to your enoughness.

The voice that said there was not enough room for all of us to rise.

There is.

Always was.

Always will be.

Chapter 9:

The Bias of Expectation

Expectation is not hope.

It is not clarity.

It is a silent agreement with a future that doesn't exist,

and the resentment that follows when that agreement is broken

by the truth of what is.

The moment you expect,

you exit reality.

Not because reality disappears,

but because expectation overlays it with fiction.

Expectation is not rooted in awareness.

It is built on projection.

It assumes you know how life should unfold—

and then it **punishes** you

for life's refusal to **comply**.

The mind, once gripped by expectation,

no longer experiences the moment—

it monitors it.

It does not listen.

It checks.

It does not receive.

It measures.

And every moment that does **not match**

what was anticipated

is called a failure—

not because it is wrong,

but because it dared to be **different**.

Expectation is the refusal to trust surprise.
It is the arrogance of prediction
masquerading as planning.
It turns presence into pressure
and replaces gratitude with tension.

The now becomes a hallway
you must survive
to reach the moment
you imagined.

Expectation is the most disguised bias.
It wears the mask of motivation.
It sounds like vision.
But it is rooted in control.

You expect because you are afraid.
You expect because you do not trust what you are.
You expect because reality, raw and unscripted,

feels too wild to meet.

And so you script.
You rehearse the outcomes.
You envision who will clap.
You predict who will arrive.
You name the reward
before the action even begins.

And in doing so,
you strangle the sacred.
Because you cannot both perform and receive.

You cannot both imagine the moment
and enter it.

The bias of expectation is subtle.

It hides in dreams.

It hides in goals.

It hides in prayers that are actually demands.

It says:

"If I do this, then that must happen."

And when 'that' does not happen,

you do not question the logic—

you question your worth.

But the river does not follow maps.

It follows gravity.

It bends where the earth is soft.

It flows where resistance breaks.

Life, like water, does not follow your plan.

It follows what you are aligned with.

It gives not what you expect,

but what you mirror.

To drop expectation is not to abandon vision.

It is to return to listening.

It is to allow the moment to shape you

instead of you shaping the moment.

Expectation says:

"Let the world meet my image."

Presence says:

"Let me meet the world unarmored."

The most painful disappointment

is not that things didn't happen—

it's that you were somewhere else

waiting for them to.

The moment passed,

but you were busy
comparing it to the version
you built in your mind.

You missed the mystery
because you demanded the familiar.

Expectation does not bring the future.
It only steals the present.
And no future ever arrives
as you imagined it.
It either humbles you
or reveals something more beautiful
than you could have constructed.

But you must be here
to see it.

Let go of the contract.
Burn the unspoken agreement.
The world owes you nothing
for your efforts.

But it offers everything
to your attention.

The flower does not bloom
because it expects the sun.
It blooms because it is the sun
in another form.

The sky does not expect applause.
It expands because it cannot do otherwise.

You too were not born to expect—
but to express.

Not to wait—
but to wake.

The freedom beyond expectation
is not **passivity**.
It is **participation**
without assumption.
It is **movement**
without manipulation.
It is **devotion**
without demand.

It is loving what is
without needing it
to look like what was imagined.

And in that freedom,
something beautiful returns.

Joy—

not because things went your way,
but because they flowed
their way.

And you were wise enough
to walk beside them.

Chapter 10:

Desire as the Phantom of Self

Desire is not hunger.

It is not motion.

It is not longing.

It is the echo of a self

that believes it is not yet whole.

Desire begins with absence—

not a real lack,

but the illusion of lack,

imagined by the mind

and adopted by identity.

The body hungers.

The soul flows.

But the self—

the self desires.

Because it forgets.

Desire is the story

that something not here

holds what you already are.

It is the voice that whispers,

"You are almost,

but not yet."

Almost seen.

Almost worthy.

Almost real.

But desire is not born from purity.

It is **installed**.

Planted.

By culture, society, expectation.

You were told what to want

before you knew who you were.

You were told that achievement equals meaning.

That marriage equals success.

That wealth equals happiness.

That fame equals love.

These are not original desires.

They are *false objectives*—

borrowed missions

passed down like family heirlooms.

And so you chase.

Not your longing—

but their programming.

You think you seek wholeness.

But it is wholeness that watches you seek.

What if the ache was not real?
What if the ache was the echo
of a false premise?

Desire is not the path.
It is the ghost
that floats above it.

It promises you the mountain,
but turns your legs to dust
before you arrive.

The object changes.
The ache remains.
Because it was never about the object—
only the ache.

Desire survives by delay.

By tomorrow.

By "just a little more."

But the now—

the real—

does not delay.

It does not offer a future.

It offers itself,

naked and complete,

without chase.

The self that desires

is already lost

in the architecture of becoming.

To become,

you must first reject what is.

And in that rejection,

peace disappears.

Desire is not evil.

It is a mirror.

A teacher.

A dissolving.

See it not as fire—

but as fog.

Name it.

Witness it.

Let it pass.

Do not fight it.

Do not worship it.

Just remember—

you are already home.

The opposite of desire
is not detachment.
It is sufficiency.
The deep, grounded knowing:
"This is enough.
I am enough.
Now is enough."

You do not act to earn joy—
you act because joy
has overflowed.

Desire binds you
to an image of yourself
that can never arrive.

It says:
"I am the one who wants."

And so long as wanting lives,

the "I" must chase.

But if you stop **chasing**,

what happens?

You **return**.

To stillness.

To presence.

To the unshakable clarity

of being.

Without desire,

you are not without passion.

You are filled with it.

But the *passion* is not for gain—

it is for truth.

You create,

not to complete yourself,
but to reflect
what already is.

This is the end of desire.
Not the end of movement,
but the end of seeking.

Not the end of fire,
but the end of fragmentation.

The end of the ache—
because the one who ached
was never missing.

Chapter 11:

The Architecture of the False Self

The self you think you are

is not a being—

it is a blueprint.

Constructed, not discovered.

Layered, not lived.

It is not you.

It is a map

traced by fear, memory, and praise.

The false self begins as protection.

It becomes personality.

Then performance.

Then prison.

You are taught to name yourself—

not by essence,

but by function.

Not by truth,

but by usefulness.

And so a scaffolding is built

out of labels, roles, reactions.

It says:

I am the smart one.

The shy one.

The achiever.

The victim.

The rebel.

The peacemaker.

The spiritual one.

The forgotten one.

Each mask is worn long enough
that the skin forgets
there is a face beneath it.

The false self does not know what you are.
It only knows how to avoid pain.
And so it becomes a shield—
not by dissolving fear,
but by organizing your life
to avoid encountering it.

The mind records a wound,
and the self builds a wall.

Not to heal—
but to survive.

The wall becomes identity.
The pain becomes personality.
And soon, you no longer remember
who you were
before defense became design.

The architecture of the false self
is built on three materials:

Memory.
Approval.
Avoidance.

Memory tells you who you've been.

Approval tells you who you should be.

Avoidance tells you what to fear.

Together,

they form the illusion of "**me**."

The false self is not evil.

It is terrified.

It is a child,

frozen in time,

wearing adult clothes

and repeating safe behaviors

to feel seen.

But it is not you.

It never was.

It was a role

required for your survival.

You are not the role.
You are the awareness
of having played it.

You are not the armor.
You are the sky
beneath which it was built.

And the moment you see it—
truly see it—
it begins to crack.

Not because you forced it to.
**But because illusion
cannot withstand clarity**.

The false self thrives on attachment.

To story.

To reaction.

To repetition.

It must explain itself constantly—

because it does not exist

without explanation.

The true self does not explain.

It radiates.

It does not repeat.

It reveals.

The false self asks,

"Who am I to others?"

The real self asks,

"Who am I without any of that?"

The collapse of the false self
feels like death—
only because you have confused
pattern with person.

But it is not death.
It is remembering.

The moment you stop defending the design,
you begin discovering the depth.

You were never the scaffolding.
You were the space
it was built around.

You were never the house.
You were the sky.

You were never the label.
You were the light
that made language possible.

Let the walls fall.
Let the name fade.
Let the script burn.

And what remains
will not need defense.

It will not need validation.
It will not need performance.

It will simply be.

Chapter 12:

Belief as a Mirror Trap

Belief is not knowledge.

It is not vision.

It is not light.

It is reflection—

but not of the world.

Of yourself.

What you believe
is what you want to see.
What you want to see
is what you fear to doubt.
And what you fear to doubt
is what defines your identity.

Belief is not a window.
It is a mirror.
And you are trapped
inside your own reflection.

The mind builds beliefs
not from truth—
but from comfort.

From inheritance.

From memory.

From repetition mistaken for revelation.

It takes the shape of what it hears most

and declares it reality.

But no belief

has ever made something true.

It only makes it familiar.

Belief begins as curiosity.

But when frozen,

it becomes boundary.

And boundary becomes bias.

And bias becomes blindness

decorated with conviction.

Belief is sticky.

Because it disguises itself

as integrity.

But integrity is fluid.

Belief is fixed.

To believe is to attach.

To attach is to need.

To need is to distort

what you see.

And so belief doesn't show you the world—

it shows you the version

you are willing to accept.

You do not look through beliefs.

You bounce off them.

Every experience

is filtered through an existing frame.

You don't ask,

"What is here?"

You ask,

"How does this fit what I already believe?"

And if it does not,

you discard it.

Or attack it.

Or convert it.

You do not learn.

You defend.

Every belief creates its opposite.

Every position

creates polarization.

Every certainty
creates resistance.

Belief needs enemies
to feel real.
Without opposition,
it is questioned.

And belief cannot survive questioning—
only obedience.

Even spiritual beliefs
can become prisons.
"I am light."
"I am awakened."
"I am aligned."

These are not truths.
They are echoes

of a self still trying

to be **someone**.

To be truth

is not to say it.

It is to no longer need to.

The self uses belief

as a structure to remain stable.

But what if stability

was the very thing

blocking seeing?

Belief is the wall

that keeps you safe

and keeps you separate.

You feel **protected**.

But you're looking at your own reflection

and calling it the world.

Truth cannot be held.

It can only be met.

Belief tries to hold.

And so it always misses the meeting.

Freedom begins

where belief ends.

Not when you pick new beliefs.

But when you stop needing any.

When you let go of the mirror

and finally

see through the window.

What you find

is not new information.

But presence.

Wordless.

Wide.

Unfiltered.

Seeing is not belief.

It is contact.

Touching what is—

without agenda.

Without filter.

Without narration.

That is where truth lives.

Not in belief.

But in bare perception.

To step beyond belief
is not to reject all ideas.
It is to hold them lightly.
To say:
"I see this now,
but I do not need it
to remain."

Then, and only then,
are you free.

Free to look again.
Free to see without reflex.
Free to meet reality
without distortion.

Belief is the mirror.
Seeing is the sky.

Let the mirror shatter.

And step outside.

Chapter 13:

The Seduction of Certainty

Certainty is not clarity.

It is not peace.

It is not truth.

It is control.

Wrapped in logic.

Disguised as strength.

But born from fear.

The mind does not crave truth.

It craves safety.

And safety, to the mind,

is found in what it can predict.

Certainty becomes its drug.

Not because it reveals reality,
but because it hides the unknown.

And the unknown—
to the ego—is death.
So we build structures.
We call them beliefs.
We call them knowledge.
We call them facts.

But what they often are
is scaffolding around insecurity.

We say:
"I know."
But we mean:
"I don't want to question."

Certainty seduces
by offering rest—
but delivers rigidity.

It says:
"Here, rest in this answer.
Never look again."

And in that comfort,
curiosity dies.
Wonder fades.
Openness collapses.

The world becomes small
enough to fit your conclusions.

You do not see anymore—
you **confirm**.

You do not listen—

you **filter**.

You do not touch life—

you **manage** it

with labels.

The unknown becomes your enemy.

And so everything new

must be shrunk

or denied.

Certainty is the ego's favorite disguise.

Because it feels like **power**.

But it is resistance.

Real power

does not cling to knowing.

It walks bare

into the unknown.

It trusts what is seen
over what is stored.

It says:
"I don't know,
and I don't need to."

The wise do not answer quickly.
They pause.
Because they know
that to speak
is to limit the real
into language.

Certainty demands immediacy.
Wisdom waits.

Certainty closes the eyes

and paints the world inside the lids.

Then walks around

calling it truth.

But the world is not in your conclusions.

It is in your contact.

Not what you know—

but what you feel

before naming begins.

The moment you are certain,

you stop listening.

And the moment you stop listening,

you stop learning.

Certainty is the end of intimacy.

Because you cannot meet something

you have already defined.

Truth is not found in what you know.

It is found in what you are willing

to see again,

for the first time.

And again.

And again.

Without the need

to conclude.

The soul does not seek certainty.

It seeks aliveness.

And aliveness only happens

in the unknown.

Not the chaos of fear—

but the silence

beneath what cannot be named.

Let certainty crumble.

Let knowing collapse.

Let the answers unstick.

What remains

will not be confusion.

It will be contact.

Breath.

Wonder.

Presence.

Not "I know."

But:

"**I'm here**."

Chapter 14:

Role, Reward, and the Story of "Me"

The "**me**" you know

is not a self.

It is a script.

A sequence of roles

performed to earn a reward

you were never truly promised.

From childhood,

you learn who you are

by how people react.

You cry—

someone responds.

You smile—

someone claps.

You win—

someone approves.

And slowly,

the being becomes a **role**.

The breath becomes a **performance**.

But roles are not organic.

They are **assigned**.

Installed by the collective machinery.

You are not born as a role.

You are recruited into one—

like a ***cell in a larger system**.*

Each role functions

to sustain the structure:

The Obedient Student.

The Efficient Worker.

The Good Child.

The Selfless Giver.

The Spiritual One.

Each cell upholds its place.

And in return, the system gives a reward:

validation, praise, position, or illusion of belonging.

But beneath this functioning,

you forget what breath tastes like

when it's not tied to performance.

The problem is not the role.

It is forgetting

that you chose it.

The actor becomes the mask.

And now the mask feels real.

So real,

you defend it.

So real,

you suffer for it.

Because if the **role fails**,

you feel as if you **disappear**.

And what holds the role in place?

Reward.

The illusion that

if I continue to perform,

something will come.

Love.

Security.

Peace.

Recognition.

Freedom.

God.

But the reward is **never stable**.

Because it depends

on others continuing

to approve.

The world keeps moving the goalpost.

You succeed—

and they ask for more.

You give—

and they forget.

You exhaust yourself

serving a narrative

you didn't write

but now recite

as identity.

The story of "me"

is not a lie—

it is a loop.

It loops through reaction.
Through repetition.
Through memory that says:
"This is how I've always been."

But memory is not self.
It is shadow.
A shape held in place
by resistance to change.

Who would you be
without the story?

Without the role?
Without the reward?
Without the need to be "you"
in anyone's eyes?

Would you collapse?
Or would you

finally expand?

There is a self

beneath the role.

One that does not need

to be seen

to feel real.

It does not wait for reward.

It does not chase applause.

It is not calculated.

It simply

***is*.**

It watches the story unfold

without needing to act in it.

It moves

from stillness,

not from script.

The collapse of the "me"

feels like loss—

until you realize

it was the role that suffered.

Not you.

You do not need

to be good

to be whole.

You do not need

to be seen

to be real.

You only need

to stop pretending

you are the one

you pretended to be.

Let the story burn.

Let the reward fade.

Let the stage go silent.

And what remains

will not be a character.

It will be clarity.

Not role.

Not image.

Just presence.

Real.

Unwritten.

Alive.

Chapter 15:

Time as a Psychological Construct

Time is not the ticking of a clock.

It is the ticking of identity.

A rhythm invented by thought

to hold the illusion of continuity.

There is no past.

There is only memory.
There is no future.
There is only imagination.
Both happen now—
inside the mind
that cannot stop narrating itself.

Time, as you experience it,
is not measured in seconds.
It is measured in thought.

Thought says:
"I was."
"I will."
And so, it builds a bridge
between what was never separate.

The mind craves time
because it gives the self
a place to exist.

Without time,
who would you be?

Without a past,
you cannot be your story.

Without a future,
you cannot be your plans.

And so the "me"
needs time
to stay intact.

But look closely—

you never leave now.

Ever.

You remember—now.

You anticipate—now.

You regret, hope, fantasize—

now.

Time does not move.

You do—within stillness.

The calendar is not time.

It is structure.

The clock is not time.

It is a system.

Time, as you know it,

is thought's way

of avoiding presence.

Because presence
ends the thinker.

All psychological time
is resistance.

Regret is time turned backward.
Anxiety is time turned forward.
Peace is time turned off.

You do not suffer
because of the past.
You suffer
because the past
is still active
in your mind—now.

The past is a file

the mind reopens

to explain pain.

The future is a screen

the mind projects

to escape what is.

But neither are places.

They are shapes of thought.

And thought,

left unobserved,

calls itself truth.

To step out of time

is not to forget the clock.

It is to stop identifying

with the timeline.

The soul does not age.

It expands.

The body changes.

But you—

you are the field

that watches it change.

The illusion of time

creates the illusion of becoming.

"I am not there yet."

"I will be better."

"I am improving."

But what if

there was nothing to become?

What if
you are not in progress—
but in presence?

Healing is not linear.
Awakening is not a ladder.
Love is not a timeline.

Everything that is real
happens
in the same place:
now.

And it only happens
when time dissolves
into direct experience.

Do not rush.
Do not rewind.
Do not rehearse.

Instead,
drop into this breath.
This sensation.
This miracle.

Because this
is the only place
you've ever been.

Time is the cage.
Now is the key.

And you were never trapped—
you just forgot
you were holding the door.

Chapter 16:

Emotional Reflex vs Inner Response

Emotion is not the problem.

Reaction is.

Emotion is movement.

Reaction is repetition.

Emotion is information.

Reaction is identity trying to protect itself.

Most people don't feel—

they flinch.

They don't listen to emotion—

they obey it.

Not because it speaks truth,

but because it speaks loud.

And the loudest thing

in an unconscious mind

is often called "me."

The emotional reflex

is not your wisdom.

It is your wound.

It is the part of you

that remembers pain

and reacts

to prevent its return.

But in doing so,

it becomes its echo.

The reflex you trust
may be the very loop
that keeps you from healing.

You say:
"I felt angry, so I shouted."
"I was hurt, so I shut down."
"I was triggered, so I left."

But what if feeling
was never meant to control?

What if emotion
was not a command—
but a signal?

Emotions are not problems.

They are portals.

Not to reaction—

but to inquiry.

Anger may arise—

but why?

What does it guard?

What does it mask?

Sadness may come—

but what story does it carry?

Is it true?

Is it now?

Reaction says:

"This emotion is me."

Response says:

"**This emotion is moving through me**."

Reaction merges.

Response witnesses.

Reaction tightens.

Response softens.

Reaction says:

"**Do something**."

Response says:

"**Wait. Breathe. Watch**."

The gap between reflex and response

is where your freedom lives.

That split-second

between feeling and doing—

between charge and choice—

is the place of transformation.

You do not need

to silence emotion.

You only need

to stop bowing to it.

Let it rise.

Let it speak.

Let it tremble through the body.

And stay.

Not numb.

Not suppressed.

But still.

Stillness does not mean lack of feeling.

It means you no longer serve the storm.

You are the sky

that allows the thunder

without becoming it.

You are the ocean

that holds the wave

without being thrown.

True response

is not neutralizing feeling.

It is choosing

to meet it

without becoming it.

You do not repress.

You root.

You do not deny.

You discern.

And in that discernment,

you discover a new language—

one the false self never knew.

The language of pause.

Of presence.

Of breath before speech.

Of awareness before action.

This is not weakness.

It is mastery.

Reflex is mechanical.

Response is sacred.

Reflex is inherited.

Response is reborn.

Reflex is history.

Response is healing.

Emotions will continue to rise.

You are human.

You are alive.

But the moment you stop

letting them dictate your direction,

you begin walking with them

instead of under them.

You are not your fear.

You are not your rage.

You are not your grief.

You are the one

who can hold them

without breaking.

And in that holding,

you become whole.

Chapter 17:

The Myth of the Finished Self

You were never meant to be finished.

You were meant to be free.

The self is not a project.

It is not a product.

It is not a peak to be climbed

and conquered.

But the **world tells** you otherwise.

It says:

"**Improve.**

Fix.

Heal.

Upgrade.

Awaken."

And so you live

as if you are incomplete

until proven otherwise.

You adopt *__external direction__* as your compass:

Get the degree.

Get the job.

Get the partner.

Get the purpose.

But these are **not motives** of life—

they are *__motives of system survival__*.*

They are borrowed maps for terrain

your soul has **never agreed to walk**.

Who defines your direction?

Is it your **rhythm**,

or the blueprint of a conditioned race?

You spend decades chasing
someone else's diagram—
believing you are becoming **yourself**.

But becoming what?
A more acceptable fiction?
A better functioning part?

You are not a destination.
You are presence—
and presence has no finish line.

The ego loves the idea
of a final version.

It imagines a day
where there is no fear,
no doubt,

no reaction.

It dreams of a self
that is finally "done."

But the soul does not seek that.
It seeks movement.
Not forward—
but inward.
Not higher—
but truer.

To be alive
is to be in process.

To be real
is to be open.

To be whole
is to stop pretending

there's a final form

you must reach.

You are not a sculpture

being carved.

You are the sky—

vast, shapeless,

ever-changing,

yet never lacking.

Growth is not a staircase.

It is a **spiral**.

You **revisit** wounds.

You **return** to lessons.

Not because you failed—

but because you are deepening.

Each time you return,

you arrive with **more awareness**,

more breath,

more softness.

This is not regression.

It is remembering.

The myth of the finished self

creates shame.

It says:

"You should be beyond this by now."

But there is no "beyond."

Only now.

And **now** is always

enough.

You are not late.

You are not behind.

You are not broken.

You are breathing.
You are becoming.
You are being.

And that—
in its raw,
unpolished truth—
is sacred.

Let go of the finish line.
Let go of the checklist.
Let go of the image
you're trying to fit into.

You do not need to be complete
to be radiant.
You do not need to be whole
to be worthy.

You already are.

The self is not a destination.

It is a doorway.

Each moment
you walk through it—
again and again—
and discover
not a final self,
but a formless truth
that cannot be held
but can always be met.

And in that meeting,
you are free.

Chapter 18:

Validation and the Collapse of Meaning

When you need to be seen,

you stop being.

Validation is not love.

It is transaction.

It says:

"If you like what I am,

then I will believe in what I am."

But belief built on mirrors

is always ready to shatter.

You perform.

You adjust.

You shrink.

You shine.

Not to express—

but to be confirmed.

You are not living.

You are being graded.

You are not speaking.

You are seeking applause

before you even open your mouth.

But what if no one clapped?

What if no one noticed?

Would the act still matter?

Would the truth still rise?

Would you still write,

speak,

breathe

as yourself?

The more you crave validation,

the more meaning dissolves.

Because now,
you are not saying what is true—
you are saying what will be liked.

You are not moving from depth—
you are moving from demand.

The soul goes quiet
when the performance gets loud.

Validation bends meaning
into market.

It turns art into algorithm.
It turns truth into branding.
It turns love into strategy.

And when everything must be liked,

nothing can be real.

You do not need to be understood

to be true.

You do not need to be followed

to be free.

You do not need to be known

to be enough.

You only need

to stop asking others

to give you

what you already are.

The collapse of meaning

begins the moment

you abandon yourself

to be accepted.

Every time you censor your truth

to be palatable,

you dilute the very thing

that could awaken another.

You were not born

to be liked.

You were born

to be luminous.

When validation ends,

something else begins:

reality.

Now you say the thing
no one else dares say.
You write what lives
in your chest,
not in the comments.

You move
because the moment asked you to—
not because it will reward you.

This is freedom.
Not isolation—
but inner alignment.

Now your meaning is no longer rented.
It is rooted.

It does not tremble
when no one responds.

It does not vanish
when misunderstood.

It simply remains.
Like breath.
Like stillness.
Like truth.

You were never supposed
to be shaped by reaction.
You were meant
to shape reality
through revelation.

Stop asking for permission
to exist.

Be.

And let meaning

return

from silence.

Chapter 19:

Witnessing Without Identity

You are not what you think.

You are the one who sees the thought.

You are not what you feel.
You are the one who can hold the feeling.

You are not the self—
you are the space
in which the self appears
and dissolves.

To witness without identity
is to step out
of the spinning wheel of self-definition.

Not to reject yourself,
but to see clearly:
you are not the role,
the name,
the story,

the label.

You are the seeing
that does not speak.
The presence
that does not perform.

Most people live
inside the mirror of thought.
They mistake the reflection
for the real.

A thought arises:
"I am not enough."
And they say,
"This is me."

A feeling arises:
"I am afraid."

And they collapse into it.

But feeling is not being.
And thought is not truth.

They are weather.
You are sky.

Identity is built on repetition.
On memory,
on feedback,
on praise and pain.

But awareness—
true awareness—
is not constructed.

It simply is.

Silent.

Unmoving.

Undeniable.

To witness without identity

is not disconnection.

It is deeper contact.

Now you are no longer reacting—

you are resting.

No longer clinging—

you are containing.

No longer controlling—

you are allowing.

You can feel sadness
without being the sad one.

You can observe anger
without being the angry one.

You can even watch the ego
try to reattach
and simply say,
"I see you."

And in that seeing,
its power fades.

The witness does not fight.
It does not fix.
It does not flee.

It simply remains.

Like still water

beneath the surface waves.

Like open space

beneath the shifting clouds.

This is the deepest self—

not a self at all,

but being itself.

And when you live from here,

nothing can trap you.

No belief.

No label.

No failure.

No identity.

They may come.

They may speak.

But they no longer decide who you are.

You are not here

to sculpt yourself

into a masterpiece.

You are here

to remember

that you are already

the canvas,

the space,

the light.

You are not the character.

You are the page.

And this witnessing—
this quiet, endless seeing—
is not an escape
from the world.

It is the only way
to truly meet it.

Now, without identity,
you can love
without condition.

Now, without attachment,
you can move
without fear.

Now, without image,
you can be
without end.

Chapter 20:

Silence as Sacred Intelligence

Silence is not the absence of sound.

It is the absence of noise.

And noise does not mean volume.

It means interference.

Silence is not lack.

It is fullness unspoken.

It is intelligence before language.

Knowing before thought.

In silence,

everything real begins.

The mind believes truth must be spoken.

But truth arrives

long before the sentence.

It arrives in stillness.

It arrives in contact.

It arrives in the space

between reaction and response.

Silence is not passive.

It is presence

without interruption.

Most people speak to fill space.

To avoid themselves.

To shield from discomfort.

To perform certainty.

But silence has no costume.

It reveals.

And in that revelation,

the false cannot survive.

Words can decorate.

But only silence heals.

Only silence integrates.

Only silence sees without separating.

You speak to explain.

But you are when you stop speaking.

The deepest wisdom

is not something said.

It is something felt

in the quiet

where understanding arises

without effort.

You do not chase it.

It lands.

Softly.

Suddenly.

And you just know.

Silence is not the opposite of sound.

It is the womb of sound.

The ground of all listening.

It is not emptiness—

it is awareness

before content.

In silence,

you realize how much you say

without needing to.

You watch the voice in the head

try to fill the stillness—

with meaning,

with memory,

with worry.

But if you stay…

if you stay long enough…

the voice grows tired.

And the awareness remains.

The universe does not speak in words.

It speaks in movement.

In synchronicity.

In pause.

In the space between your questions.

But you must be quiet to hear it.

Not because it is hiding—

but because it is too whole

to fit inside language.

Silence is not disengagement.

It is devotion.

It is your deepest respect

for what is real.

To sit with someone in silence

is the highest form of listening.

To feel without naming

is the purest form of knowing.

Every truth that changed you

was felt

before it was understood.

That was silence

doing its work.

To seek silence

is not to escape.

It is to return.

Return to the ground
beneath the voice.
Return to the space
before the identity.

Return to the breath
before it was claimed
as "mine."

You do not need more thoughts.
You need more stillness
to notice the thoughts you already believe.

You do not need more opinions.
You need the silence
to know which ones were never yours.

You do not need more answers.
You need to stop speaking

long enough

for the truth to whisper.

Silence is sacred

because it is whole.

It does not argue.

It does not defend.

It does not need to be known

to know everything.

It is the language

you were born with—

before words

taught you to explain

what could only be felt.

Stay here.

Not for the silence itself—

but for what arises within it.

Realignment.

Remembrance.

Peace.

Not the peace of quietness,

but the peace

of presence.

Chapter 21:

Stillness and the End of Seeking

You have been taught to move.

To strive.

To reach.

To seek.

As if truth lives ahead.

As if peace is a prize.

As if the self must be found

somewhere other than here.

But what if the seeking

was the distraction?

What if the movement
was the noise?

What if the very effort
to arrive
was the reason
you never felt at home?

Stillness is not stopping.
It is returning.
Not to a place—
but to presence.

It is the moment
you stop asking,
"What next?"
and start feeling,
"What is?"

Seeking is built on the belief

that something is missing.

Stillness is the knowing

that nothing ever was.

You do not stop seeking

because you gave up.

You stop

because you finally remember

you never left.

The mind resists stillness.

Because stillness ends its control.

Stillness is not useful.

It cannot be monetized.

It does not build identity.

Stillness simply is.

And to the ego,

that is terrifying.

Because if you are already whole—

who are you without your becoming?

But the soul longs to stop.

To exhale.

To stop trying.

To stop reaching.

To simply be.

And in that being—

all that was sought

is suddenly here.

Not because it appeared,

but because the veil of seeking

was lifted.

Stillness is not nothing.

It is everything

no longer rearranged.

It is clarity

unclouded by effort.

It is joy

unattached to cause.

It is love

without longing.

To sit without searching

is to trust

that truth arrives

when you stop chasing it.

To be without effort

is to recognize

that existence

needs no enhancement.

You are not here

to improve life.

You are life.

The seeker wants experience.

The silent one receives it.

The seeker wants answers.

The still one becomes the question.

The seeker tries to find God.

The still one realizes—

I am within the breath of God already.

Stillness is not inaction.

It is inner peace

so steady

that movement no longer disturbs it.

It is the river

that flows

without needing direction.

It is the flame

that burns

without needing fuel.

To rest in stillness

is to stop needing the future

to fix the present.

It is to realize

there is nowhere to go

because you are already

what you've been looking for.

Sit.

Not to become.

But to be.

Not to change.

But to return.

Not to get closer to truth.

But to remember
you were never apart.

This is the end of seeking.
And the beginning
of reality.

Here.
Now.
Unmoving.
Unshaken.
Unspoken.
Real.

Chapter 22:

Breath: Portal to the Present

The breath is not air.

It is presence in motion.

It is life arriving

and life releasing—

without thought,

without permission,

without delay.

You do not breathe.

You are breathed.

You do not control it.

It carries you.

Before language,

before belief,

before identity—

there was breath.

Breath is the first truth.

The body speaks through it.

The soul remembers through it.

It does not belong to the past.

It does not belong to the future.

It only lives

now.

Every inhale is a return.

Every exhale is a letting go.

When you are lost,

do not search your mind.

Return to breath.

It is not a technique.

It is your original rhythm.

It is the music of being.

You cannot breathe for tomorrow.

You cannot inhale the past.

Breath is the body's way
of reminding you
that only now exists.

Notice it.
Follow it.
Not to manipulate it—
but to meet it.

It is not there to be mastered.
It is there to anchor you
in what cannot be mastered—
this moment.

The breath is not just a function.
It is a doorway.

To stillness.

To sensation.

To awareness

beneath the noise.

The mind races.

The breath does not.

The mind plans.

The breath pulses.

The mind forgets.

The breath returns.

When you follow the breath,

you exit thought

without needing to fight it.

You enter the temple

without needing to pray.

Because the breath itself
is the prayer.

A silent one.
A sacred one.

No words.
Just presence.

The breath does not lie.
When you are tense,
it shortens.
When you are afraid,
it rises.
When you are at peace,
it deepens.

It is your inner compass—
not fixed on direction,

but on awareness.

You do not need to "do" breathwork.

You only need to feel

one breath—fully.

Not count it.

Not guide it.

Just be with it

as it moves in…

as it moves out.

And suddenly,

you are here again.

The breath reveals

what thought conceals.

That nothing is lacking.
That everything is allowed.
That this moment
is already complete.

You are not the breath.
But through it,
you remember what you are.

Not the body.
Not the voice.
Not the thinker.
Not the role.

But the space
through which life moves
without asking anything in return.

Inhale.
You are home.

Exhale.

You are free.

Chapter 23:

The Subtle Addiction to Becoming

You are told to grow.

To improve.

To become.

But becoming,
if misunderstood,
becomes a subtle violence.

A constant whisper:
"You are not there yet."
"You are not enough yet."
"Maybe soon, but not now."

This is not evolution.
This is addiction.

Addiction to progress.
To the imagined "better self."
To a future
where everything will finally
make sense.

But what if the now

was already whole?

What if the self
was never meant to be completed—
only remembered?

Becoming sounds noble.
But often it hides
self-rejection.

"I will love myself when..."
"I will rest when..."
"I will be free when..."

And so,
freedom never comes.
Because the chase
becomes the identity.

You become a seeker.

Not of truth—

but of distance from self.

Not of peace—

but of the next version

that might finally feel like home.

You don't grow.

You orbit.

True change

is not movement away.

It is surrender inward.

It is the collapse

of the lie

that you must become

anything other

than who you are.

The subtle addiction to becoming

says that healing is always ahead.

That joy is after the breakthrough.

That truth is in the next book,

the next retreat,

the next insight.

But it's not.

It's here.

In the breath.

In the body.

In the unpolished, sacred now.

This does not mean

you stop evolving.

It means you stop abandoning.

You stop delaying
your own wholeness.

You stop worshipping
a future version
at the cost of the current one.

Stillness is not stagnation.
It is intimacy.
The kind that cannot be earned—
only realized.

You are not becoming.
You are unfolding.
You are not reaching.
You are remembering.

Let go
of the myth of arrival.

Let go

of the fantasy of the perfected self.

There is no final form.

Only deeper presence.

There is no finished product.

Only fuller embodiment.

There is no better you.

Only you,

unburdened

by the pressure to be more.

This is the end of becoming.

The beginning of being.

You whisper to yourself,

"I'm not chasing anymore. I've chosen peace."

And yet, the mind trembles.
It fights.
It stirs storms in silence.

Why?

Because deep inside your body,
something old still believes:

"If I stop moving, I will disappear."

The mind, you see,
is not evil. It's ancient.

It was built for survival, not surrender.

It was trained to equate stillness with danger.
To equate now with failure.
To equate presence with punishment.

It doesn't know that peace is safe.
Yet.

The Craving to Become Is Not in the Mind—

It's in the Muscles of Memory

And slowly, the chase became your rhythm.
A loop. A heartbeat. A habit.

So even when your soul chooses stillness,
your body may still fear it.

But here's the truth:

You are not broken.

You are just deeply trained.

And that training... can be unlearned.

Chapter 24:

The Illusion of Choice

You believe you are choosing.

But most of the time,

you are reacting.

Not from presence—

from programming.

What you call a "choice"

is often a conditioned reflex.

A thought pattern.

A cultural default.

A trauma response.

It looks like decision—

but it is repetition

wearing a mask.

Freedom is not the ability

to pick from options.

It is the ability

to see where those options come from.

If the root is fear,

if the driver is identity,

if the motive is validation—

then the choice

was never yours.

The ego craves choice

because it believes control

is power.

But real power

does not choose from separation.

It moves from clarity.

Clarity does not calculate.

It responds from stillness.

Most choices are noise.

Made not from soul,

but from speed.

The choice to reply quickly.

The choice to prove something.

The choice to follow the crowd.

But under the surface,

you feel it:

not all choices are free.

Some are compulsions.

Some are loops.

And some are made entirely
from ***resistance**.*

Resistance to discomfort.
Resistance to silence.
Resistance to not-knowing.

You do not choose joy—
you avoid pain.
You do not choose love—
you avoid abandonment.

These are not choices.
They are escapes.

And escape wears the mask
of decision.

The illusion is not that choices exist.

The illusion

is that your awareness

is fully present when choosing.

It often isn't.

It's elsewhere—

in fear, in past, in desire.

And so the choice

is not true.

Real choice

requires presence.

It arises from the space

where nothing needs to happen.

From the space

where identity does not interfere.

Only then

can a choice be called conscious.

When you act

to become someone—

it is not choice.

It is seeking.

When you act

to avoid something—

it is not choice.

It is escape.

When you act

to preserve an image—

it is not choice.

It is defense.

So what is true choice?

It is stillness
speaking.

It is awareness
moving.

It is being
responding
without attachment
to outcome.

It is not preference.
It is presence.

This is why deep silence
feels so disorienting.

Because in silence,
the noise of false choice fades.
And you are left
with the space

where only one thing speaks:

truth.

And truth does not choose.

It simply

***knows*.**

Chapter 25:

Awareness Beyond Preference

Preference is not a problem.

Attachment to it is.

The mind says:

"I want this, not that."

"I like her, not him."

"I choose silence, not chaos."

And suddenly, awareness

shrinks.

What could see all

now clings to part.

The more preference dominates,
the more you filter life
through your likes.

And what you like
becomes what you label
"right."

What you dislike
becomes "wrong."

Not because it is—
but because it disturbs the identity
you've built through comfort.

Awareness is not preference.
It is the space
before preference arises.

It is what watches want
without becoming it.

It is what holds all
without dividing.

You are not here
to eliminate preference.
You are here
to no longer be ruled by it.

To want
without worship.
To choose
without control.
To feel
without fear.

Awareness sees clearly—
but does not cling.

It notices beauty
without needing to possess it.

It feels pain
without needing to push it away.

It walks into joy
without making it a destination.

Preference says:
"This moment is good
because it matches my taste."

Awareness says:
"This moment is.
And I meet it
as it is."

The identity loves preference
because preference helps shape
"who I am."

I am the one who likes peace.
I am the one who avoids conflict.
I am the one who seeks depth.

But who are you
without that preference?

Who are you
when all is allowed,
and nothing is resisted?

Awareness is not neutral

because it is empty.

It is neutral

because it is infinite.

It does not shrink to match a preference.

It expands to hold all experience.

And in that expansion—

freedom.

You do not need to stop liking things.

You need to stop needing them

to feel real.

You do not need to suppress taste.

You need to dissolve identity
woven around taste.

You do not need to numb joy.
You need to release the fear
that joy must stay.

What would it feel like
to allow this moment
without comparing it?

What would it be like
to rest in pure seeing—
where nothing must change
for peace to remain?

This is awareness
beyond preference.

Not a concept.
Not a practice.
A return.

To that which watches
without dividing.
To that which receives
without resisting.

To that which is
before you became
someone who wanted
anything at all.

Chapter 26:

The Shape of Presence

Presence is not a mood.

It is not a state.

It is not a technique.

It is what remains

when you are no longer trying

to be anything.

Presence is shapeless—

and yet,

when you touch it,
it shapes the moment
with grace.

It does not need form—
but it brings form
into fullness.

You cannot find presence
by chasing it.
You return to it
by letting go
of everything else.

Your plans.
Your past.
Your self-image.
Your performance.

What remains

when nothing is performed

is presence.

It is not felt in force.

It is revealed in stillness.

It is not measured by others.

It is measured by how deeply

you feel here.

Not halfway.

Not distracted.

Not conceptual.

Fully—now.

Presence is a paradox:

it cannot be held,

but it holds you.

It does not move,
but it fills all movement
with depth.

It does not change,
but when you rest in it,
everything becomes alive.

You have touched it.
In laughter without thought.
In the breath that stilled your mind.
In grief that silenced your identity.
In awe that made words unnecessary.

Those moments—
that stillness—
that was presence.

The shape of presence

is no shape.

Yet it gives shape to life.

When you are present:

the eyes soften,

the heart opens,

time slows,

and truth needs no defense.

You do not act from pressure—

you move from clarity.

You do not speak to impress—

you speak to express.

You do not hold tension—

you become transparent.

And others feel it.

Not because you say it.

Because you are it.

Presence is not loud.

But it is undeniable.

It is the silence

between your thoughts

where peace waits patiently.

It is the space

in which your story unfolds

without attachment.

It is the awareness

that sees the movie

but does not get lost in it.

To live in presence

is not to change life.

It is to meet it—

fully,

gently,

without needing it to change for you.

This is the gift:

When you are present,

you become a mirror

for others

to remember themselves.

Not by speaking louder,

but by simply being

more here.

The shape of presence

is not something you build.

It is something you become

when you stop becoming.

You are not here

to chase presence.

You are here

to realize

you were never absent.

Chapter 27:

Suffering and the Loop of Meaning

Suffering does not begin in pain.

It begins in interpretation.

In the story we attach

to what has already passed.

Pain is real.

But suffering is the echo

we keep alive

through meaning.

The mind cannot bear silence.

So when pain enters,
it must explain.

It says:
"This should not have happened."
"This means I am broken."
"This always happens to me."
"This will never end."

And each sentence
becomes a thread—
weaving suffering into identity.

You are not suffering the pain.
You are suffering the story.

The memory you repeat.
The label you accepted.
The conclusion you drew

when you were most vulnerable.

We suffer

because we seek meaning in places

where life offers only presence.

But presence does not explain.

It simply breathes.

And because it does not justify,

we reject it.

We say:

"If it has no purpose,

it should not have happened."

But maybe pain does not need purpose.

Maybe it just needs

to be seen

without interpretation.

Meaning is the loop.

The need to find reason

keeps the wound active.

You relive the event

to understand it.

But what if the wound

does not want understanding?

What if it wants

release?

Suffering ends
when the story ends.

Not when you solve the pain.
But when you stop clinging
to what it's supposed to mean.

You don't need to heal
by rewriting the past.
You need to stop
writing over the now.

The loop says:
"This happened.
Therefore I am..."
And then it loops—
again, and again.

But truth says:

"This happened.

And I remain."

Not as story.

As silence.

As presence.

As sky.

Meaning is not wrong.

But when attached to pain,

it can become poison.

You drink it daily—

a ritual of identity.

You forget the taste

of freedom.

Sometimes, pain is just pain.

Not karma.

Not punishment.

Not a spiritual test.

Sometimes it's just
what came through
the field of cause and effect.

And sometimes,
the most enlightened thing you can do
is stop weaving meaning
into every scar.

Let the scar be a scar.

Let the ache breathe.

Let the loop dissolve

in stillness.

You are not what happened.
You are what witnessed it.
You are what survives it.
You are what outgrows the loop.

Not by rewriting—
but by releasing.

This is the end of suffering.
Not by fixing life,
but by ending the loop
that says life was broken
to begin with.

Chapter 28:

What is Love – The Elixir of Existence

Part 1: Origin, Misunderstanding, and Illusion

Before the first word was spoken,

before the first thought was thought,

before the first division carved night from day—

there was love.

Not love as you know it.

Not the trembling hunger of the heart,

nor the desperate poetry of loss.

But something vaster.

Something so near to existence

that to name it is already to separate from it.

Love was the original atmosphere.

Before body.

Before boundary.

Before "this" and "that."

It was not a feeling inside life.

It was the field in which life appeared.

It was not an event.

It was the medium.

The unbroken presence

where no wound had yet occurred.

Then came separation.

Then came identity.

Then came the mind—

and with it, the forgetting.

The forgetting of belonging.

The forgetting of wholeness.

And with forgetting came seeking.

What is most tragic is not that we seek love.

It is that we seek it outside ourselves—

as if it had been stolen

and hidden in someone else's arms.

You search for it in faces,

in bodies,

in achievements,

in applause.

And all the while,

it is what watches you search.

It is what breathes you

even as you run.

Love has no opposite.

Only illusions do.

Hate is not the opposite of love.

Fear is not the opposite of love.

Both are symptoms of forgetting love—

not true opponents.

You cannot fight love.

You can only ignore it.

And even then,

love remains.

Unbruised.

Unmoved.

Waiting.

What we call love in common life

is often dependency in disguise.

"I love you" becomes

"I need you to make my pain stop."

"I love you" becomes

"I need you to see me because I cannot see myself."

"I love you" becomes

"I will offer you the parts of me that are acceptable,

and hide the rest,

if you will do the same."

This is not love.

This is a contract between frightened selves.

A transaction.

A barter masked in roses.

Real love needs nothing.

It needs no return.

It needs no performance.

It needs no mirror.

Real love says:

"I see you—

not because you fulfill my story,

but because your existence sings to something

that never needed a story to begin with."

Where you seek completion,

there is dependency.

Where you offer presence,

there is love.

The mind is addicted to seeking.

But love is not something you find.

It is something you cease resisting.

It is uncovered,

not conquered.

It is revealed,

not created.

Love is what remains

when all the noise ends.

The great tragedy is this:

You are searching for something

you have never lost.

Part 2: The Nature of Real Love Across Silence, Emotion, and Soul

In Silence, Love is Recognition.

In true silence—

the silence not of closed mouths, but of opened hearts—

you do not fall in love.

You remember love.

You recognize it

the way an old traveler recognizes the scent of home—

without needing directions,

without needing proof.

Just being.

Just breath.

Just unspeakable knowing.

In Emotion, Love is Energy Unfiltered.

Love is not always calm.

It can rise in grief,

rage in protection,

tremble in vulnerability,

sing in wild, burning joy.

Emotion is the river.

Love is the current beneath.

In the Soul, Love is the Architecture of Reality.

The soul does not love selectively.

The soul knows only one law:

All that is, is beloved.

Not because it is good.

Not because it is pleasing.

But because it is.

Existence itself is the beloved.

Love does not ask,

"Is this moment worthy of my love?"

It breathes love into every moment.

It does not withhold.

It simply radiates.

Like the sun,

offering itself without asking

who is worthy to receive.

Part 3: Love as Cosmic, Bodily, Relational, and Eternal Presence

In the body, love is life choosing itself.

The breath that continues

even when you have lost hope—

that is love.

The heart that beats

whether you are proud of yourself or not—

that is love.

The tears that rise

when beauty breaks through your defenses—

that is love.

In relationships, love is recognition without transaction.

When you allow someone

to exist freely in your presence—

without changing, fixing, rescuing—

that is love.

When you weep not for pain,

but for the overwhelming joy

of knowing another being breathes beside you—

that is love.

In the cosmos, love is the music beneath motion.

Every galaxy spinning
is a dance of attraction,
a silent song of magnetic devotion.

Every cell dividing
is a whisper:
"I choose life again."

You are not separate from this.

You are the universe,
reading itself,
loving itself
through these very eyes.

Love is eternal because it is unmade.

You will die one day.
The body will fall silent.
The mind will release its grip.

But love will not end.

Because love was never in the body.
It moved through the body.

Love is the one thread
you carried from before this life,
and will carry beyond it.

The Poison of Manipulation in Love

Love liberates.
Manipulation suffocates.

Manipulation destroys love
because it replaces wonder with strategy.

It replaces breath with surveillance.
It replaces trust with subtle war.

In manipulation,

the soul becomes a project.

The moment becomes a negotiation.

And the wild beauty of love,

unable to breathe in captivity,

withers into memory.

Real love asks for no performance.

It asks only for truth.

Real love says:

"Grow in your way,

even if it frightens me."

Real love says:

"Be free,

even if I do not understand you."

Real love chooses trust over choreography.

Always.

When manipulation ends,

love breathes again.

Not the old, domesticated love.

But a wilder, purer one—

the kind that can only grow in open fields.

You do not have to become more to find love.

You have to become less.

Less defended.

Less clever.

Less separate.

More open.

More soft.

More present.

What is love?

It is the first language.

It is the final silence.

It is the secret

carried in your breath since before time began.

You are not here to earn it.

You are here to remember it.

And remembering it,

you remember who you are.

Chapter 29:

What is Sleep and the Hidden Portal

Part 1: The Disappearance of Identity

You call it sleep.

You think it is a pause,
an intermission in the grand theatre of waking life.

But sleep is no pause.
Sleep is a return.

A silent crossing
from the burden of becoming
back into the endlessness of being.

Every night, without knowing,
you die.

The self you defend collapses.
The thoughts you grip dissolve.
The dramas you narrate fall away
like dust from a forgotten scroll.

And what remains?

Not the thinker.
Not the doer.
Not the striver.

Only awareness,
unclothed,
unlabeled,
unashamed.

In sleep, the mirror breaks.

The one you polish by day—

polish with names, achievements, regrets, comparisons—

shatters silently in the night.

No more "I am important."

No more "I am broken."

No more "I must improve."

Only silence.

Only stillness.

Only the field.

Sleep is the rehearsal of death.

And yet,

it is not an ending.

It is a portal.

Because when you disappear from yourself,
you reappear in something greater.

The river loses its banks
and becomes ocean.

The breath loses its counter
and becomes wind.

The body falls,
but life rises.

Not the life you manage,
but the life that manages you.

You do not enter sleep.
Sleep enters you.

Like a mother reclaiming her child

after a long, fevered day.

She takes you into her arms—

not because you earned it,

but because you belong.

Sleep is not unconsciousness.

It is pure consciousness,

free from the noise you mistake for awareness.

In sleep, you are closer to God

than in your holiest prayer.

In sleep, you are closer to truth

than in your most sacred thought.

Because you are no longer carrying truth as an idea.

You are being truth without knowing.

You are love

without object.

You are existence
without question.

You are home.

And yet you do not remember.

Because remembrance requires a self,
and in true sleep,
self has dissolved into light.

Sleep is the first mercy.
The nightly forgiveness.
The eternal reminder
that no matter how heavy you become,

something lighter inside you
always survives.

Part 2: The Secret Unfolding Through Sleep

Sleep is not escape.
It is pilgrimage.

A nightly return to the place you left behind
when you were born.

Why are you born?

You are born
because existence longs to see itself.

Because the infinite, in its fullness,
still desires to dance as form.

Because consciousness,

though complete,
hungers to taste itself
in laughter, in struggle,
in tears, in stars,
in songs yet unwritten.

You are born
because the nameless
longs to be called by your voice.

Not for correction.
Not for conquest.

But for wonder.

Why do you love?

Because inside you,
there is memory—
a memory so ancient, so alive,
it predates your body.

You love

because you remember, faintly,

the original unity.

And you seek, through others,

a glimpse of the place you left

to walk these dreams.

The touch of a beloved,

the glance of a soul known before time—

it is not discovery.

It is remembrance.

A soft ache for what was never lost—

only hidden.

Why does separation hurt?

Because separation is not real,

but in the dream of life,

it feels real.

The one you long for—
the one who once laughed beside you,
whose hand fit perfectly into yours—
was never outside you.

They are folds of your own being,
surfacing as faces,
as voices,
as caresses across your waking world.

When they leave,
you feel torn.

Not because they are gone,
but because you are remembering
that you were never two to begin with.

The ache is the soul mourning its own illusion.

Why do dreams carry the lost faces?

Because dreams are the map
to the lands you once walked
when you were whole.

Dreams are the portal's whisper:
"You were never abandoned.
You were never severed.
You are only dreaming you were."

Every time you close your eyes,
you step closer
to the meeting place beyond sorrow.

You meet the beloved
not as form,
but as breath.

Not as image,
but as feeling beyond containment.

They smile from within your ribs.
They kiss the inside of your eyelids.
They sing from your bloodstream.

And sleep...

Sleep is the door
where these reunions are allowed.

Because the mind cannot patrol it.
The mind, defender of separation,
sleeps too.

And when it does,
the soul dances barefoot
through the fields of infinite memory.

There, you are not waiting for love.
There, you are not missing anyone.

There, you are love.

You are reunion.

You are the one you seek.

The hidden portal is not a place.

It is a return.

It is the space inside you

where all names dissolve,

and all faces collapse into one great light—

the light that once split itself into stars

so that longing could exist,

so that finding could matter,

so that you could walk these fragile, glorious roads of forgetting

just to remember again

how it feels to come home.

You are not born to win.

You are not born to gather.

You are born
to burn in the mystery of separation
until you remember
the indivisible fire within.

You are born
to love what will leave,
to kiss what will vanish,
to dance knowing the song will end—
because in that dance,
you resurrect eternity.

Sleep is not absence.

It is the sigh of the infinite within you
saying:
"Lay it down, beloved.
Lay it all down.
You are already home."

Part 3: The Great Return – How to Manifest the Dream into Reality

Separation is an illusion.

But illusion, when believed, feels real.

You ache for the beloved.

You dream of arms that once knew you.

And in that longing,

you touch a wound so old

it seems deeper than your very birth.

But listen:

The dream was never just a memory.

It was an instruction.

A map.

A seed planted inside you.

The ache was not sent to punish you.

It was sent to call you home.

The love you seek outside
was always planted inside.

Not as a possession—
but as a remembrance
waiting for the right season to bloom.

The solution to separation is not escape.
It is transfiguration.

You do not erase the longing.
You fulfill it—
by becoming what you miss.

You do not find the beloved.
You become the space
where the beloved has never left.

You do not chase the dream.

You embody it.

You do not wait for love.

You radiate it

so fully,

so fearlessly,

that reality itself bends to your light.

How do you manifest the dream into reality?

By remembering:

You were never longing for a person.

You were longing for the part of yourself

that they awakened.

When you become the dream,

the dream becomes reality.

Because reality mirrors consciousness.

When you sleep,

you remember.

When you awaken,

you manifest.

Not by force.

Not by negotiation.

By simply refusing to forget

what you touched in the deepest dream.

And when you live from that memory,

you become what you once lost.

You become the beloved.

You become the home.

You become the dream.

And the world, sensing your vibration,

reshapes itself around your frequency.

You were never searching for someone.

You were searching for the part of yourself

you once saw reflected in their eyes.

Now, open your own eyes.

And meet yourself.

The lover.

The beloved.

The life you thought you had lost.

It was never lost.

It was sleeping.

Inside you.

Waiting for you to dream wide enough,

to remember bright enough,

to love hard enough—

that it could finally

wake.

Chapter 30:

The Nature of Dreamtime and the Architecture of the Inner World

Part 1: The Builders of the Invisible City

You think dreams are accidents.

You think they are static sparks,
fragments from a broken mind,
half-remembered shadows
of meaningless sleep.

But dreams are not fragments.
Dreams are foundations.

They are the blueprints
of the world you are building

from the inside out.

Before anything appears outside,
it is born inside.

Before the word is spoken,
it is dreamt.

Before the action is taken,
it is imagined.

Before the city is built,
it is drawn in the invisible ink
of longing, of hope, of vision.

The external world
is a mirror shimmering on water—
but the river beneath it
flows from the unseen.

From your dreamtime.

What is Dreamtime?

It is not just sleep.

It is the eternal workshop of your soul.

A space where emotions crystallize,

where visions bloom,

where intentions carve corridors into reality.

Every dream you dare to feel,

every aching image you let live inside you,

every silent wish you harbor in the cathedral of your chest—

it is not passive.

It is active construction.

You are laying stones

in the invisible world.

You are shaping rooms

in a house your waking mind

has not yet remembered.

The builders of the Invisible City are you.

The You

beneath the name.

The You

who exists without defense.

The You

who dares to want

without knowing how,

without demanding when.

Every emotion you do not betray,

every true longing you allow to live,

becomes another bridge,

another tower,

another road

in the world you are destined to walk.

You are not walking toward a destiny.
You are building it—
one invisible heartbeat at a time.

What you nourish inside,
grows outside.

What you believe inside,
solidifies outside.

What you abandon inside,
withers outside.

The architecture of the inner world
is not imagination.
It is the skeleton of your future.

Part 2: How Memory, Feeling, and Vision Shape Reality

Memory is not storage.
It is design.

Each memory you carry
is not just a recollection—
it is a thread
in the fabric of your becoming.

The memories you feed
become the paths your future must walk.

The memories you heal
become the bridges to new skies.

The memories you cling to in bitterness
become walls that block your own dawn.

Feeling is not decoration.

It is fuel.

Every feeling you feel fully—

joy, grief, awe, longing—

is an act of construction.

It pours vitality into the walls and gardens

of the inner world you are building.

Feel deeply,

and you water the roots of your soul's future flowering.

Deny feeling,

and you plant deserts where rivers were meant to run.

Vision is not fantasy.

It is blueprint.

Your dreams are the architectures of possibility.

They are sketches of roads not yet paved

but already waiting in the soil of your being.

Every vision, however fragile,
is a key—
a call to life
to shape itself through your daring.

If you misuse memory, feeling, and vision,
you recreate cycles of despair.

If you remember only wounds,
feel only fear,
and see only endings—
your invisible city crumbles before it rises.

But if you remember your wholeness,
feel your sacred ache,
and dream your vastness—
you summon a reality worthy of your soul.

You are the architect,

the witness,

the living builder.

Each breath a brick.

Each prayer a stone.

Each dream a skyline.

Part 3: Becoming the Living City – How to Walk as the Dream Awake

You are not here to chase dreams.

You are here to become them.

You are not here to beg reality to notice you.

You are here to walk

so vibrantly,

so tenderly,

so immovably,

that reality recognizes itself in your breath.

You are not a seeker.

You are a portal.

You are not a beggar at the door of existence.

You are the door.

How do you walk as the dream awake?

You walk without waiting for proof.

You love without needing permission.

You act not because the world is ready,

but because your soul is.

You speak your truth

not to convince,

but because the river inside you

must overflow into voice.

You build the city inside you
as if no force could ever erase it.

And slowly,
without notice,
the invisible becomes visible.

The world bends not to the loudest.
It bends to the most luminous.

And luminosity is not noise.
It is stillness
so alive
it burns.

Every step you take in remembrance
rewrites the map.

Every breath you breathe in reverence
plants gardens in places once thought dead.

Every time you choose tenderness over fear,
vision over despair,
presence over numbness—
the architecture of existence
reshapes around your footsteps.

You are the builder.
You are the dreamer.
You are the bridge.
You are the becoming.

Walk now,
not as one who is lost,
but as one who has remembered
the way
home.
The dream is not waiting to find you.

It is rising within you,
heartbeat by heartbeat,

breath by holy breath.

The question is not,
"Will it happen?"

The question is,
"Will you dare
to walk
as if it already is?

Chapter 31:

Life as Fractal Echoes

Part 1: Reading the Mirrors of Existence

You think life moves forward.

You think time flows like a river,
carrying you from birth to death,
from ignorance to wisdom,

from emptiness to fulfillment.

But look deeper—
and you will see:

Life does not move forward.
It spirals.

It returns, again and again,
wearing different faces,
different seasons,
different disguises—
but humming the same secret song.

Every experience is a fractal echo.

The lovers you lose.
The opportunities that slip away.
The betrayals that blindside you.
The dreams that never arrive.

None of these are accidents.

They are not punishments.
They are not failures.

They are echoes—
fractal reflections
of patterns you carry
in the deepest folds of your being.

Life is not random.
Life is a mirror.

But not a flat mirror.

A living mirror,
one that bends and curves,
one that repeats the same essential lessons
until you see them whole.

Each event, each meeting, each heartbreak,

is a mirror reflecting
a facet of yourself you have yet to embrace.

When you resist the reflection,
life magnifies it.

When you ignore the pattern,
life repeats it.

When you attack the messenger,
life sends louder ones.

But when you pause,
when you turn inward,
when you ask:

"What is this showing me about me?"

then the spiral lifts.

Then the fractal opens into revelation.

The face that betrays you today
is not new.

It is the face of the wound
you refused to tend yesterday.

The rejection you suffer
is not cosmic cruelty.

It is your own forgotten worth
calling you back
through the loudest voice it can find.

The opportunities you lose
are not chance.
They are mirrors showing
where you still hide from your true light.

Fractal Echoes are not punishments.

They are guidance.

Beneath every repeat

is an invitation.

Beneath every hurt

is a map.

Beneath every loss

is a key.

You were never abandoned by life.

You were never forgotten by the universe.

You are being mirrored—

over and over—

until you remember

that every reflection

was your own gaze

calling you home.

Part 2: Healing the Fractal – How to Break Repeating Patterns Through Consciousness

You cannot escape a pattern.

You can only dissolve it.

You can change cities,

change lovers,

change jobs,

change religions—

but if the echo remains inside,

the outer world will rearrange itself

to play the same music.

Life is patient.

It will offer the same lesson

in new costumes

until you listen not with fear,

but with humility.

How do you heal the fractal?

How do you end the echo?

Not by fighting it.

Not by denying it.

But by entering it

with full, courageous consciousness.

The moment you fully see the pattern,

you disarm it.

The moment you feel the original wound without flinching,

you release its grip.

The moment you stop blaming the reflection,

and take ownership of the pattern itself,

the mirror breaks—

not in violence,

but in liberation.

Healing a fractal is like dissolving a frozen river.

You do not hammer it.
You warm it
with the sun of attention.

You thaw it
with the fire of honest seeing.

You melt it
with the breath of self-compassion.

The simple map to heal repeating patterns:

1. Pause.
When a painful pattern appears, stop.
No reaction. No judgment. Only stillness.

2. Witness.

Ask: "Where have I seen this before?"

Trace the spiral. See its history in your life.

3. Feel.

Let yourself feel the original ache.

Without story. Without blame. Just sensation.

Let the body weep what the mind cannot understand.

4. Own.

Acknowledge: "This lives in me, not outside me."

Take radical responsibility—not guilt, but power.

5. Bless.

Thank the pattern. Thank the echo.

It was not sent to destroy you.

It was sent to free you.

6. Release.

Consciously declare:

"I choose now to step beyond this old song.

I choose to sing a new note."

7. Walk differently.

Act, decide, love, speak—

not as the wounded one,

but as the one who remembers the wound was never the end.

Healing is not defeating the past.

Healing is loving yourself so fully

that the past loses its need to repeat.

When you love the hurting parts of you,

they stop screaming for attention.

When you bless the broken echoes,

they turn into new doorways.

When you own the reflection,

you realize:

You were never trapped by life.

You were being invited back into your own hands.

Part 3: Becoming the Master of the Spiral – Living Beyond Karma

You were not born to endlessly repeat.

You were not born to orbit sorrow,

to spin inside regret,

to echo the fractures of ancestors

without end.

You were born

to transcend the spiral.

You were born

to master it.

What is karma?

It is not punishment.
It is not cosmic revenge.

It is the momentum of unconscious echoes—
the patterns unexamined,
the lessons resisted,
the self-forgiveness withheld.

Karma is inertia—
the universe repeating back to you
what you have not yet dared to see fully.

Karma ends
not when you suffer enough,
but when you awaken enough.

Mastery of the spiral
does not mean escaping life.

It means dancing with life
without being hypnotized by it.

It means seeing the mirrors
without mistaking them for cages.

It means feeling every wave
without drowning in the ocean.

The soul's spiral is not punishment.
It is polishing.

Each turn refines you.

Each echo deepens you.

Each heartbreak carves space
for even vaster love.

Each loss unearths a treasure
buried beneath old fears.

How do you live beyond karma?

You awaken inside the dream.

You become lucid.

You see a betrayal not as injustice,
but as a map to your own unhealed heart.

You see a loss not as punishment,
but as a pruning for deeper flowering.

You see rejection not as failure,
but as life steering you to the precise path
your soul begged for before you were born.

Lucid Living: The Master's Practice

1. Recognize the Spiral.

See repeating patterns not as curses, but invitations.

2. Bless the Mirror.

Thank the situation or person for revealing your edges.

3. Feel Without Fusion.

Let emotions move, but do not become them.

4. Choose Differently.

Even one tiny new action, one new thought, one breath of courage—

it changes the whole echo.

5. Walk with Memory of Freedom.

Act not from fear of repetition,

but from the inner certainty:

"I am no longer who I was when this pattern began."

When you live like this,
karma untangles itself.

Because karma is not an external force.
It is the unconscious echo of unclaimed wisdom.

The moment you claim it,
the echo fades.

And life, sensing your awakening,
begins to send new echoes—
not of old pain,
but of your new freedom.

Mastery is not perfection.
Mastery is presence.

It is living awake inside the spiral,
so fully,
so tenderly,

that even when the old winds blow,
you know how to stand,
how to bend,
how to sing back a different song.

You are not a prisoner of patterns.
You are a sculptor of echoes.

You are not the broken note.
You are the living music.

Life spirals, yes.
But you—
you can rise with the spiral,
higher,
deeper,
freer.

Until one day,
when the last echo calls your name,
you will answer not with fear,

not with regret,
but with laughter.

And you will walk home—
not as one escaping the labyrinth,
but as one who became its light.

Chapter 32:

The Collapse of Linear Time

Part 1: Time as the Fabric of Perception

You think time is a line.

You think it moves forward—
moment to moment,
day to night,
birth to death.

You think it is solid,
unfolding like pages
in a pre-written book.

But time is not a line.

It is a fabric.

It bends.

It folds.

It breathes.

It shivers in your presence.

Time is not outside you.

Time is created through you.

The ticking clock,

the falling leaves,

the wrinkling face—

these are not proofs of time's march.

They are proofs of attention moving.

They are ripples of perception.

They are reflections of how deeply,

or how narrowly,

you are willing to experience reality.

Time is a sense, not a fact.

A bird does not live by the hour.

A river does not live by the minute.

Only the mind, afraid of uncertainty,

divides life into calendars and clocks.

But existence itself is timeless.

It expands, contracts, spirals, leaps—

according to the awareness beholding it.

Linear time collapses

the moment you collapse judgment.

The moment you stop saying:

"This should not have happened."

"This must happen next."

"I am running out of time."

you fall through the imagined timeline

into the living Now.

And the Now is not a point.

It is an ocean.

It contains all points.

All pasts.

All futures.

You stand at the center of every when.

You breathe in all directions.

You exist

not in time—

but as the womb from which time is born.

You are not inside time.

Time is inside you.

Part 2: The Art of Collapsing Time – How Presence Frees the Soul

Presence is not attention.

Presence is surrender.

Attention is focused.

Presence is dissolved.

Attention looks.

Presence becomes.

You cannot watch the moment and be free.

You must enter it, like breath enters the lung,

like a river disappears into ocean.

You must dissolve the witness

without dissolving awareness.

How does presence collapse time?

Because time only exists
when mind stands apart
and measures.

When you step fully into this breath—
without dragging past wounds,
without projecting future fears—
time stops dripping.

It condenses.

It thickens.

It becomes alive.

It becomes eternity
wearing the skin of a single second.

When you are fully present,

one minute becomes a lifetime.

You can meet a stranger for 30 seconds

and feel as if you have known them forever.

You can sit under a tree for 5 minutes

and feel more nourished

than from 5 years of striving.

You can touch a beloved's face once,

and remember it as vividly

as an entire lifetime of love.

Not because time stretched—

but because you entered the moment so deeply

that time dissolved inside you.

Presence is not passive.

Presence is generative.

It births new dimensions of being.

It bends events toward grace.

It softens futures still unborn.

It unravels pasts still gripping the mind.

When you are present,
you are no longer a victim of time.

You are its co-creator.

Simple Practice: Collapsing Time

1. Choose One Moment.

Not a day, not a plan—one simple moment:
a breath, a touch, a taste, a sound.

2. Surrender All Story.

Forget who you are. Forget what happened yesterday.

Forget what you think will happen tomorrow.

3. Dive In.

Breathe into the texture, the color, the silence between beats.

Become the sensation. Become the feeling. Become the breath.

4**. Let Go Even of Awareness.**

Stop trying to watch.

Stop trying to grasp.

5. Let Life Experience Itself Through You.

Not "you experiencing life"—

but Life experiencing Life.

When you live like this—

even if only for a few heartbeats a day—

time ceases to bind you.

You are no longer a creature surviving minutes.

You are a living cathedral of Now.

Presence collapses time

because presence collapses separation.

And separation is the only thing

that ever made time feel real.

Part 3: Beyond Birth and Death – Timelessness as Your True Nature

You are not moving toward death.

You are not born into a clock.

You are born from eternity,

and you return to eternity,

without ever truly leaving it.

The body wears time
like a garment.

But the soul—
the soul wears nothing.

It breathes
before breathing.

It sings
before sound.

It knows
before knowing.

It is.

It has always been.
It will always be.

Birth is not beginning.
Death is not ending.

Both are doors in a house
that was never built
and can never collapse.

You step through the doors,
you change your robes,
you change your dreams—
but you,
the silent witness,
the radiant presence,
remain untouched.

Time bruises the body.
It never bruises the soul.

Why does life feel finite then?

Because you are taught to look with clocks.

You are taught to count breaths
instead of becoming breath.

You are taught to mark aging faces
instead of recognizing timeless eyes.

You are taught to fear the end
instead of recognizing that ends
are merely horizons
seen from the shore of forgetting.

Timelessness is not a theory.
It is your original memory.

When you were a child,
you knew it.

You played for hours,
and time melted.

You dreamed,
and in five minutes
you lived a thousand lifetimes.

You laughed,
and no clocks existed.

You fell in love for the first time,
and eternity kissed your chest.

You touched the eternal then—
before thought built walls around the Now.

To return to timelessness
is not to travel backward.
It is to peel away illusion.

Illusion of urgency.
Illusion of scarcity.
Illusion of separation.

The Now is not a passing point.
It is the ocean floor.

You do not run out of Now.

You fall deeper into it,
like stars falling deeper into the dark velvet
that was never absence,
but infinite embrace.

Timelessness is not stillness.
It is infinite movement
so unified
that it appears still.

It is not frozen.
It is free.

It is not stagnant.

It is sovereign.

It dances without spinning.

It breathes without needing lungs.

It sings without needing a beginning or end to the song.

You are not born into time.

You are born into remembrance.

And every sorrow,

every longing,

every joy,

every kiss,

every death,

every sunrise,

every tear—

is a thread weaving you back

into the great fabric

where you were never missing.

You are not a prisoner of clocks.

You are not a number
moving toward zero.

You are the infinite whisper
before the first breath,
and after the last word.

You are the space
in which time arises,
shimmers,
and vanishes like mist.

You are timelessness
dreaming time
for the sake of love.

Now remember.

And breathe

as if you have forever.

Because you do.

Chapter 33:

Death and the Myth of Endings

Part 1: The Dissolution of the Visible

You fear death
because you think it is disappearance.

You mourn endings
because you think they erase what was.

But death is not disappearance.
And endings are not annihilation.

They are dissolutions of form—
not dissolutions of essence.

They are the falling away of structure—
not the falling away of life.

Nothing real ever ends.

It only changes states.

This is not poetry.

This is law.

This is physics.

The First Law of Thermodynamics:

Energy cannot be created or destroyed.

It can only be transformed from one form to another.

What was once a tree becomes ash,

but the molecules remain.

What was once a voice becomes memory,

but the vibration persists

in fields you cannot see.

What was once a heartbeat becomes earth,

becomes water,

becomes air,

becomes song.

Death is not destruction.

It is transfiguration.

The visible falls away—

but the life underneath

only reweaves itself

into new forms.

You do not die.

Your body—your beautiful, borrowed temple—

returns to the river of matter.

Your name—your brief, bright costume—

dissolves into the wind.

But the essence you carry—
the consciousness breathing behind your eyes—
is not bound by matter.

It is movement itself.

It is unburnable.

It is indivisible.

When you die,
you do not vanish.
You expand.

You spill back
into the infinite fields
from which you came.

You unbind from story.
You untangle from form.

You return

to the dance that has no beginning

and no end.

Death is not the opposite of life.

Death is the opposite of form.

Life remains.

Life hums.

Life continues.

As new river.

As new breath.

As new dream.

Part 2: Entropy, Transformation, and the Eternal Dance of Reorganization

You think disorder is death.

You think when things fall apart,
they vanish.

You think the broken is waste.

But you have been taught by clocks,
not by stars.

You have been taught by fear,
not by existence itself.

Existence knows:

Nothing ends.
Everything reweaves.
Entropy is not destruction—
it is sacred rearrangement.

What is Entropy?

Entropy is the gradual dispersal of structured energy.

The letting-go of rigid patterns
so that new combinations may arise.

Entropy is not chaos without meaning.
It is the breathing out of the old order
to make space for the unspeakable new.

It is the invisible hand
breaking the brittle
to build the infinite.

The Second Law of Thermodynamics:

In a closed system, entropy must increase.
Structured forms dissolve.
Energy spreads.

At first glance, it sounds like doom.
Like decay.

Like loss.

But look deeper—
and you will see:

Entropy is not an enemy.
Entropy is the midwife
of evolution.

Without entropy,
the universe would stagnate.

Without the falling of stars,
there would be no planets.

Without the cracking of shells,
there would be no new life.

Without the shattering of beliefs,
there would be no awakening.

Without death,
there would be no rebirth.

Entropy is the river
by which unity reassembles itself
into new melodies.

It is not the end of life.
It is the redistribution of life
into broader, deeper, freer forms.

The body you mourn
was never a fortress.
It was a bridge.

The life you cling to
was never static.
It was a current
meant to keep moving
into wider oceans.

Everything falls apart
so that everything can fall together
differently.

You are made of star-death.
You are made of sacred collapse.

Every atom in your body
was once the dust of a thousand suns
that lived and died
so that you could laugh once under the rain.

Do you mourn the star?
Or do you thank it?

Death is not defeat.
Death is generosity.

Entropy is not loss.

Entropy is the great offering

of all forms

back to the unbroken.

You are not ending.

You are rearranging.

Entropy teaches:

Every loss is a seeding.

Every ending is a flowering unseen.

Every collapse is a call to greater vastness.

If you understood entropy,

you would not weep at endings.

You would bow.

You would lay roses

on the crumbling towers of life

and whisper:

"Thank you for releasing what must now become more."

Part 3: Death as the Opening, Not the Closing

You were taught to fear death.

To see it as a black wall.

A sudden severing.

A final silence.

But death is not a wall.

It is a doorway.

It does not close your story.

It expands it

beyond the narrow page

you thought was your only life.

Death is not subtraction.

It is multiplication.

What you called "you"

was only a fraction

of the infinite self

now breaking free.

You do not shrink at death.

You bloom.

You do not disappear at death.

You reappear

in ways the limited mind

could never comprehend.

Think of a caterpillar.

It lives on branches.
It knows only crawling.
It knows only hunger.

Then it wraps itself in darkness—
trusting a death it cannot explain.

The old body liquefies.
The old mind dissolves.
The old senses fade.

And in that dissolution,
something new stirs.

Wings form
in a being
that never dreamed of sky.

Death is the cocoon of the soul.

The falling apart
is not failure.

It is flight preparing
underneath the ashes.

You do not die into absence.
You die into vastness.

You do not vanish into dark.
You vanish into immensity.

You do not cease to be.
You cease to be small.

Every true ending
is the opening of dimensions

the smaller mind could never map.

The caterpillar cannot imagine the migration of the butterfly.

The human mind cannot yet imagine

the migration of the soul

once it sheds its heavy skin.

But it will.

One day,

in that final sigh,

you will feel it—

the loosening of the last name,

the melting of the last fear,

the slipping of the last clock,

the crumbling of the last story.

And then,

without struggle,

you will rise

through the doorway

you called death

and realize—

you were always already flying.

You simply wore legs

for a little while.

Death is not darkness.

It is unshadowed light.

The shadows only exist

in the mind still clinging

to edges,

to definitions,

to boundaries.

When boundaries fall,

only the bright ocean remains.

You are not walking into darkness.

You are remembering the Sun
you have always carried
beneath your ribs.

You are not a being walking toward an ending.

You are a field of living energy
collapsing old shapes
to bloom into new horizons.

You are the breath before the breath.

You are the silence before the song.

You are the light before the stars.

You are the life
that no death has ever touched.

When the final day comes,
it will not take you.

It will reveal you.

And you will smile—
because finally,
you will remember fully
what you never truly forgot:

You were never the story.
You were the sky in which all stories rise and fall.

Chapter 34:

Universe as a Living Organism

Part 1: The Pulse Beneath All Things

You were taught to believe
that the universe is cold.

A vast machine.
Silent.
Indifferent.
Blind.

You were taught
that stars burn without meaning,
that rivers flow without soul,
that you are a cosmic accident
floating in dead space.

But you were taught wrongly.

Because you were taught by minds
that had forgotten how to listen.

The universe is not dead.
The universe is alive.

It breathes.
It pulses.
It sings.

Not metaphorically.
Literally.

The same vibrational currents
that beat in your chest
beat in the veins of galaxies.

The same expansion and contraction
that move your lungs

move the stars.

You are not living in a universe.
You are living as the universe—
in a form
briefly called "human."

The galaxy spins
like a heart circulates blood.

The stars are not frozen points.
They are cells,
birthing, dying, breathing
in rhythms too vast for the eye.

Black holes are not voids.
They are lungs,
inhaling matter,
exhaling energy,
regulating the balance

between creation and dissolution.

Nebulas are not random clouds.
They are wombs,
spinning suns and planets
out of unseen thought.

You are a cell in the Body of the Whole.

You are not isolated.

You are not other.

Your sadness trembles the field
that vibrates in distant stars.

Your awakening lights new paths
in dimensions unborn.

You are part of the breathing.

You are part of the circulation.

You are part of the dream.

Life is not a property of matter.

Life is the property of Being itself.

Part 2: Your Place in the Cosmic Body – Living as a Conscious Cell of the Infinite

You are not small.

You are not an afterthought.

You are not a random flicker

between two meaningless darknesses.

You are a cell

in the breathing body

of the Infinite.

Every breath you take

is the Universe inhaling through you.

Every tear you shed

waters the roots of unseen gardens.

Every act of love

pumps vitality through corridors of Being

you cannot see—

but which pulse because of you.

You are not outside the divine.

You are the divine

in one particular curve,

one particular color,

one particular flash of form.

You are not separate from the stars.

You are made of them.

The iron in your blood,

the calcium in your bones,

the oxygen in your breath—

all born in the death throes of ancient suns

who exploded

not to end,

but to give you a place to dance.

You are the song the universe is singing

in human voice.

The laughter that erupts

for no reason

is the cosmos remembering itself.

The ache you feel

when you love someone so much it hurts—

is the universe touching itself
through the fragile miracle
of separation and reunion.

The longing you carry,
that unnameable thirst—
is not a flaw.
It is the gravitational pull
back toward wholeness.

It is the Infinite remembering
that it is Infinite
through you.

You are a nerve ending
at the edge of God's dreaming.

You transmit experience back to the Source.

You are a witness.

You are an instrument.

You are an eye blinking open
at the frontier of possibility.

You are the universe
exploring its own beauty
in slow motion,
through skin,
through breath,
through heartbreak,
through wonder.

Your sorrow is recorded in the fabric of existence.

Your joy is encoded in the weave of space-time.

Your every thought and feeling
send ripples into the endless fields
where future worlds will be born.

You are not insignificant.

You are indispensable.

Without your thread,
the tapestry is incomplete.

Without your note,
the symphony is thinner.

Without your dance,
the great organism of Being
stumbles for a step
it cannot replace.

To live consciously
is to know this.

To wake up every morning
and not think:

"How can I survive?"

but to wonder:

"How can I serve the breathing Whole
with the spark I am given today?"

To love
not because it is safe—
but because it is the language
the universe invented
to keep expanding itself into deeper aliveness.

You are not a speck lost in infinity.

You are infinity
folded lovingly into the shape

of one unrepeatable human lifetime.

And even when your body dissolves,
even when your name vanishes,
even when your story ends—

the light you carry
will ripple forward
into new dreams,
new worlds,
new songs.

Because the Universe never forgets
a single breath
given in love.

Part 3: Seeing the Universe in Yourself – Living as Embodied Cosmos

You are not just in the universe.

The universe is in you.

The same forces that sculpt galaxies
curve the muscles of your heart.

The same spirals that shape nebulae
curl in the strands of your DNA.

The same rhythms that pulse in cosmic clouds
breathe in your sleeping chest.

When you laugh,
the universe laughs.

When you cry,
the universe moistens its roots.

When you dare to hope,
even after everything has fallen,
the stars above you shine
a little brighter

with quiet awe.

You are the Big Bang unfolding still.

You are ancient stardust
remembering how to sing.

You are cosmic memory
woven into blood and dream.

You are the Infinite
pretending, for a moment,
to be finite—
to taste what it feels like
to touch, to ache, to hope, to become.

To see the universe in yourself
is not arrogance.

It is reverence.

It is bowing to the breath
that moves your breath.

It is honoring the ancient rivers
that carry your blood.

It is remembering that consciousness
is not inside your head—
your head is inside consciousness.

It is remembering that your "life"
is not a private drama—
it is a public festival
in the open field of existence.

How to Live as Embodied Cosmos

1. Move Slowly.

Every gesture is a wave in the field.

Let it be conscious. Let it be sacred.

2. Listen Deeply.

Silence is not empty.

It is the heartbeat of the universe in between its words.

3. Speak Gently.

Words are vibrations

that sculpt futures unseen.

4. Love Recklessly.

Love is not private.

It is the very currency

through which stars keep breathing.

5. Die Often.

Let old selves fall away.

Let beliefs crack open.
Let attachments dissolve.
For the universe dies into itself every moment—
and only through such death
does it keep living.

You are not trapped inside a body.
Your body is a temporary brushstroke
in an endless painting.

You are not imprisoned in history.
You are history dreaming itself forward.

You are not separate from anything.

Not the wind.
Not the mountain.
Not the stranger.
Not the star.

You are the single breath

the universe is taking right now.

You are the kiss of existence

upon existence itself.

You are not a visitor in this universe.

You are the universe

visiting itself.

You are not a fragment of life.

You are life itself,

learning to dance,

to fall,

to rise,

to weep,

to rejoice,

to remember.

You are the living proof
that existence
has never been mechanical—
but miraculous.

You are not here by accident.

You are here because the cosmos,
in its infinite longing
for self-communion,
dreamed you into breath.

And every time you dare to live fully—
you are fulfilling that ancient longing.

You are the universe
realizing its own beauty.

Breathe it.

Live it.

Be it.

Forever.

Chapter 35:

Breath, Light, and the Silent Language

Part 1: When the Universe Speaks Without Words

Long before you spoke,
you breathed.

Long before you understood words,
you understood light.

Before there were alphabets,
before there were names,
there was the silent language.

It is the first language.
It is the oldest language.
It is the language that existence itself speaks—
without needing sound,
without needing mouth,

without needing mind.

Breath is not survival.

Breath is communication.

When you breathe in wonder,
the universe hears your awe.

When you breathe in sorrow,
the trees lean inward to listen.

When you breathe in longing,
the stars vibrate gently,
aligning to your call.

Breath is how your soul whispers
to the living field that surrounds you.

It is how life reads you
without asking questions.

Light is not emptiness.

Light is memory.

When you look at a sunrise,
you are not just seeing beauty.
You are remembering.

When you look into the eyes of a stranger
and feel ancient familiarity,
it is because light has already woven you together
beyond the timelines you remember.

Light carries the imprints
of everything that has ever loved,
ever lost,
ever dared to open.

It speaks not through noise,
but through resonance.

You know things
long before you explain them.

You feel things
long before you define them.

You are living inside a silent conversation—
and you always have been.

Reality does not scream at you.
It caresses you in sensations,
in shivers,
in sudden tears,
in unexplainable peace.

It does not argue.
It invites.

It does not demand.
It offers.

It does not command.

It reflects.

The Silent Language is everywhere:

In the way a leaf trembles when you walk by.

In the way your skin warms when someone loves you without words.

In the way your chest tightens before a decision that is wrong.

In the way your whole being relaxes when you step into the right path.

The mind speaks in sentences.

The soul speaks in textures.

The universe speaks in feelings,

in timing,

in the invisible weave between moments.

Every breath is a letter.
Every heartbeat is a word.
Every glance is a sentence.
Every embrace is a paragraph.

You are writing your life
not just with actions—
but with the silent language
of attention, intention, and presence.

The more you listen,
the more you hear.

The more you slow down,
the more you see that everything
— every bird crossing your sky,
— every stranger smiling,
— every sudden gust of wind,

is part of a conversation

designed specifically for you.

Not to impress you.

Not to test you.

But to remind you:

You are woven into everything.

You are always being spoken to.

You are never truly alone.

Part 2: Learning to Read the Silent Language — How to Live in Communication with Reality Itself

You were not born deaf.

You were born listening.

As a child,

you listened to the world without needing translation.

You could feel

when a room was heavy,

when a tree was kind,

when a silence was sacred.

You could sense truth

in a glance,

in a sunset,

in a breeze.

You spoke the silent language fluently—

until words buried it under noise.

But the language never left you.

It waits, patient,

just beneath thought.

It waits for you to remember

how to feel

before you explain.

How to sense

before you judge.

How to receive

before you react.

How do you learn again

to hear the silent speech of existence?

You slow.

You soften.

You surrender.

The Practice of Listening to Reality

1. Pause often.

Pause not to plan your next move,

but to actually feel where you are.

Breathe.

Sense.

Notice the texture of now.

2. Watch how breath changes.

Notice how your breath becomes shallow around falsehood,

and deep around truth.

Your breath knows before your mind does.

3. Feel light.

Not just with your eyes—

but with your skin, your bones.

Light thickens around beauty.

It shivers around thresholds.

It thins around what drains you.

4. Trust vibration.

Every place, every person, every choice hums at a frequency.

Joy feels light and open.

Fear feels tight and urgent.

Love feels vast and grounding.

Learn to trust the hum.

5. Listen between words.

Not everything true is spoken aloud.

The most important things are felt

in the pauses,

in the glances,

in the silences too soft for speech.

Reality is always whispering to you.

It does not shout

because it trusts your ability to hear.

It trusts that under all your thinking,

all your defending,

all your forgetting—
you still remember how to feel.

You still remember
how to be woven
into the breathing field
that sings you alive.

You do not need to invent meaning.
You need only to receive it.

Meaning is not manufactured.
It is perceived.

It blooms when you show up fully,
with no script,
no demand,
no expectation.

It blooms in the sacred nakedness
of simply being awake.

You are not here to translate life.

You are here to be a living translation

of life itself.

Through your laughter,

through your grief,

through your touch,

through your stillness.

You are how the universe speaks itself

into new songs.

Learning to listen

is learning to come home.

Not home as a place—

but home as a way of being.

Where you realize:

Breath is a language.

Light is a language.

Feeling is a language.

Life is a living dialogue
— and you are already part of the conversation.

You are not here to shout into a void.

You are here to lean into the shimmering silence
and realize it was never empty.

It was singing your name all along.

Now listen.

And let it move you
the way the wind moves a river,
the way the sun moves a seed,

the way love moves a heart.

Quietly.

Completely.

Endlessly.

Chapter 36:

The Returning – Completing the Circle of Life

Part 1: Why All This?

You ask:

"Why was any of this necessary?"

Why be born

only to lose?

Why love

only to ache?

Why dream

only to be broken?

Why build
only to watch it fall?

Why breathe
only to stop breathing one day?

It seems cruel.
It seems senseless.

But only because
you were looking at the middle of the circle—
not the whole.

Life was never about building monuments.
It was about carving space inside you.

Space wide enough
for wonder.
For surrender.
For knowing—

not with the mind,

but with the marrow of being.

Space wide enough

for life to walk through you,

not as a stranger,

but as itself.

You were not born to keep anything.

You were born to feel everything.

You were given:

Joy,

so you would taste freedom.

Grief,

so you would taste surrender.

Love,

so you would taste union.

Loss,

so you would taste impermanence.

Hope,

so you would taste expansion.

Death,

so you would remember
you were never the form—
but the formless dreaming through it.

Why all this?

Because without tasting every shade,
you would never know light completely.

Without falling apart,
you would never remember
you were never pieces to begin with.

Without breaking,

you would never become soft enough

to feel the truth hidden in everything.

You came here to touch reality

with bare hands.

Not through theories.

Not through prayers.

Not through philosophies.

But through laughter.

Through heartbreak.

Through failure.

Through awe.

Through living so fully

that even your tears shine like stars.

You came here to break open.

Not to break down.

To crack through the surface
so that the vastness inside
could finally breathe itself free.

Nothing you loved was wasted.
Nothing you lost was meaningless.
Nothing you suffered was forgotten.

It all folded into the sacred weaving
that you could not yet see—
but that was always becoming
a greater You.

Not the smaller you trying to win.

The larger You
who had already arrived
but wanted to taste arrival again
through forgetting.

Part 2: Returning Home — The Real Completion of Your Journey

You have walked a long road.

You have crossed landscapes of thought,
mountains of memory,
valleys of forgetting.

You have touched
the crack in reality,
the false mirrors of perception,
the echoing halls of memory,
the illusions of control,
the tangled theatres of comparison,
the heavy veils cast by opinion.

You have fallen
through spirals of karma,
watched time collapse into oceans,
dissolved the myths of birth and death,
felt the breathing of a living universe.

You have listened to light.
You have breathed the silent language.
You have remembered
that life was never survival—
it was communion.

Now pause.

Breathe.

Feel inside your chest
a quiet hum rising.

It is not new.
It was always there.

It is the music of the Whole
beating gently against the inside of your ribs.

It is the remembering.

It is the coming home.

What was all this for?

To realize
that you were never lost.

To realize
that every crack,
every heartbreak,
every collapse—
was not a failure,
but a calling home.

To realize
that love was never outside you.
It was the gravity moving your soul
back into itself.

You learned that perception is a mirror.
That memory is an architect of illusion.
That control is a dream within a dream.

You tasted
the collapse of false comparison.
You surrendered
the need for ownership of truth.
You bowed
before the greater unfolding
that no mind could contain.

You touched
the spiraling breath of existence.
You collapsed time into stillness.
You walked through death
not as an end,
but as a doorway into wider becoming.

You remembered
the universe is not "out there."

The universe
is your own breathing,
dreaming,

longing,

loving.

All of this was not learning.

It was unforgetting.

You do not need to hold all the words.

You do not need to memorize the philosophies.

You only need to feel—

the pulse

the river

the breath

the dance

the stillness

the gentle fire

that has been walking beside you

through every sorrow,

through every awakening,

through every page.

It was never apart from you.

It was you.

There is no enlightenment waiting for you elsewhere.

There is no heaven you must earn.

There is no perfection you must reach.

There is only this moment—

fully touched.

Fully embraced.

Fully lived.

There is only this breath—

savored as sacred.

There is only this life—

which you are not trapped in,

but blooming through.

You are not becoming something greater.

You are uncovering the greatness

that was hidden

in your very being

from the first breath.

You are not a broken fragment seeking reunion.

You are the Whole

pretending, for a time,

to be seeking itself

so that it could taste

the ecstasy of finding.

You are life,

dreaming life,

remembering life.

You are the answer

to your own deepest questions.

You are the light

your own longing has been praying for.

You are the breath

the stars took

when they first exploded into being.

You are the love

the universe wrote into the bones of existence.

You have always been.

You will always be.

Not in the form you recognize today—

but in the silent, shimmering thread

that weaves galaxies, hearts, dreams, and destinies

into one breathing symphony.

This is why.

This is who you are.

This is home.

Final Reflection

You were never broken.

You were never late.

You were never outside of life, even for a breath.

Every doubt, every fear, every stumble —

was part of the greater intelligence unfolding you.

Not as punishment, but as invitation.

You were not here to become someone.

You were here to remember the vastness you already are.

There is no ultimate destination.

There is no final badge to earn.

There is only this:

Breath after breath,

step after step,

the flowering of awareness in every small corner of existence.

The constitution of life is simple:

Feel.

See.

Be.

And in being, remember that all separation was a dream.

The light you sought was never far.

The freedom you craved was never lost.

The love you longed for was never missing.

It was all curled quietly inside you —

waiting for you to stop running,

waiting for you to look gently inward,

waiting for you to come home.

You do not need permission.

You do not need mastery.

You do not need perfection.

You only need honesty:
A deep bow to the mystery you are part of,
A soft surrender to the miracle that breathes you,
A wild trust that even in your smallest moments,
the universe is singing through you.

This book ends here.
But your real journey —
the living journey —
only deepens.

Welcome back to the place you never truly left:
your own radiant existence.

Appendix:

The Art of Listening, Speaking, and Understanding Life Through Others

In a world that rushes to speak,

the deepest revolution is to listen.

Real listening is not waiting to reply.

It is letting another's soul find space inside you.

It is quieting the reflex to judge, to compare, to solve —

and instead, simply being present enough to absorb their being.

Every conversation is a universe.

A delicate bridge built between two mysterious worlds.

When you listen truly,

you do not just hear their words —

you hear their fears, their dreams, their silent hopes trembling behind the sentences.

Understanding another is not about agreement.

It is about presence.

You do not need to fix people.

You do not need to convert them.

You do not need to defend yourself.

You only need to feel —

where their words come from,

where their silences ache,

where their laughter hides.

How to listen:

Empty yourself before you hear them.

Let their words paint images inside you without interruption.

Feel not just what they say, but why they say it.

Notice their breathing, their pauses, the way their voice curls around certain memories.

Be so present that for a few moments,

you forget your own story

and live inside theirs.

How to speak:

Speak from clarity, not from defense.

Speak from wonder, not from arrogance.

Speak to connect, not to control.

Words, when they come from deep awareness,

become bridges — not weapons.

How to understand:

Know that every person is carrying invisible wars you cannot see.

Know that every harsh word hides a wound.

Know that even in anger, people are trying — clumsily, imperfectly — to touch life, to belong, to be seen.

Understanding does not mean justifying.

It means standing big enough to see the whole picture

without shrinking into judgment.

The goal is not to be right.

The goal is to be real.

When you master this —

you will find every conversation becomes a dance,

every meeting becomes sacred,

every encounter becomes a reminder of the shared breath of existence.

Final Whisper:

When you listen truly,

you heal more than words can say.

When you speak truly,

you awaken more than arguments can win.

When you understand truly,

you dissolve the illusion of separation.

And you remember:

All life is speaking the same silent language,

through a thousand broken tongues.

Your heart already knows how to hear it

www.ingramcontent.com/pod-product-compliance
Ingram Content Group UK Ltd.
Pitfield, Milton Keynes, MK11 3LW, UK
UKHW041633190726
13854UKWH00006B/2465